FACILITATING
ADULT
LEARNING

FACILITATING ADULT LEARNING

A Transactional Process

Edited by
Michael W. Galbraith
Temple University

KRIEGER PUBLISHING COMPANY
MALABAR, FLORIDA
1991

Original Edition 1991

Printed and Published by
KRIEGER PUBLISHING COMPANY
KRIEGER DRIVE
MALABAR, FLORIDA 32950

Library of Congress Cataloging-in-Publication Data
Facilitating adult learning : a transactional process / edited by
  Michael W. Galbraith.
    Includes bibliographical references.
    Contents: The adult learning transactional process / Michael W.
Galbraith—Grounding teaching in learning / Stephen Brookfield—
Individualizing the teaching and learning process / Burton Sisco,
Roger Hiemstra—Paradigms for critically reflective teaching and
learning / Victoria J. Marsick, Karen E. Watkins—Adult learning
methods and techniques / Michael W. Galbraith, Bonnie S. Zelenak—
Technology for teaching and learning improvement / Constance C.
Blackwood, Barbara A. White—Evaluating the teaching and learning
process / Paulette T. Beatty, Linda L. Benefield, Lani J. Linhart—
Strategies and resources for improving the instructional process /
Ralph G. Brockett.
    ISBN 0-89464-370-3
    1. Adult education—United States. 2. Learning. I. Galbraith,
Michael W.
LC5251.F33 1990
374'.973—dc20   90-31853
                                                              CIP

10 9 8 7 6 5 4 3 2

To T.J.

Contents

Preface

The concept of facilitating adult learning has been interpreted in various ways. For some individuals, it will be described in metaphoric terms such as a journey or transformational adventure in which the facilitator is viewed as a guide, mentor, resource person, coach, counselor, or helper for the exploration of some newfound intellectual territory. For others it is envisioned as an equal partnership between teacher and learner in an educational encounter. Still others interpret the concept of facilitating adult learning to mean the teacher takes a more controlling and authoritative stance in the pursuit of helping adults learn, with learners engaging in less collaborative and proactive activities. This has led to ambiguity and contradiction as well as the idea that one primary instructional process exists that can be utilized with all adult learners in all educational settings. Facilitating adult learning is a very complex process that incorporates diverse paradigms of thought. It requires an understanding that facilitators and learners bring into an educational encounter varying personalities, shifting expectations, diverse learning styles, personalities, personal and professional experiences, levels of sophistication, and various cultural and ethical backgrounds. In addition, institutional settings in which the learning takes place as well as the social and political climates contribute to the complexity of the total process. It should be recognized that different approaches are necessary within the teaching and learning process because of the diversity, variability, and varying levels of expectations of the learners, the subject matter presented, and the varying intellectual domain levels of the learners. Predictability is not something that characterizes the teaching and learning process; more realistically it is unpredictability.

The central purpose of *Facilitating Adult Learning: A Transactional Process* is to present one specific approach to understanding the teaching and learning process and to view this process as a transaction. The process is characterized by elements of collaboration, challenge, reflectivity, action, respect, freedom, and equality. It invites facilitators and adult learners to think and act differently and to discover new meaning to their experience. The transactional process purports that how we teach is intimately related to why and what we teach. A fundamental assumption is that by understanding the essential elements and alternatives to the teaching and learning process, facilitators and adult learners can make the experience a more joyous, rewarding, and cooperative journey.

The audience for this book includes those involved in adult and continuing education, human resource development, higher education, and vocational education settings. For those familiar with the various paradigms of thought relating to adult learning, it will provide additional information and perhaps generate a need to reevaluate and reconceptualize the teaching and learning process. For those unfamiliar with the subject, the book provides a wealth of information, strategies, and resources in which to understand its dynamics and complexity.

Facilitating Adult Learning: A Transactional Process has eight chapters. In the opening chapter, I explain the characteristics and descriptive features of the adult learning transactional process. Essential elements of the process such as truth, responsibility for our actions and learning, openness to challenge, and risk taking are examined. A discussion follows on the characteristics, roles, and skills of the facilitator of adult learning. The chapter concludes with the presentation of six guiding principles of the adult learning transactional process and how they apply to the teaching and learning encounter and to the way learning activities are designed and implemented.

In Chapter 2, Stephen Brookfield explores the concept and approach of grounding teaching in learning. He suggests that teachers of adults can be more effective if they become aware of how learners experience learning. Brookfield reports how interviews, learning journals, and critical incidents can elicit from learners their perceptions of the learning process.

Burton Sisco and Roger Hiemstra in Chapter 3 describe a comprehensive instructional system, referred to as the individualized instructional process, that is designed to be flexible, practical, and applicable in a variety of educational settings. The authors offer a model for organizing instruction in an individualized manner and give examples of how the individualized instructional process works. They discuss common issues instructors may face in using the process.

Chapter 4 examines paradigms for critically reflective teaching and learning. The authors, Victoria Marsick and Karen Watkins, use metaphors (the machine, the organic system, and the brain) to examine some of the paradigms that have governed views of learning and the implications these metaphors have for understanding the role of the facilitator. Critically reflective learning is examined through these related approaches—action science, reflection-in-action, and action learning. A discussion on the skills needed to be an effective facilitator of critically reflective learning concludes the chapter.

Adult learning methods and techniques that complement the adult learning transactional process and adhere to its essential characteristics are discussed in Chapter 5 by myself and Bonnie Zelenak. The seven methods and techniques examined are discussion, simulation, learning contracts, inquiry teams, case method, critical incident, and mentoring.

In Chapter 6, Constance Blackwood and Barbara White comment on the use of educational technology as an enhancement to the teaching and learning transaction. A variety of available technologies which feature an interactive component are examined as well as the instances in which identified technologies are most effective. Their chapter concludes with some detailed ideas on the future of instructional technology in adult education.

Evaluating the teaching and learning process is the focus of Chapter 7. Paulette Beatty, Linda Benefield, and Lani Linhart present a framework for thinking about the evaluation of instruction and the central issues associated with it. The authors offer practical strategies and guidelines that can be employed in the design of an effective evaluation plan.

In the final chapter, Ralph Brockett provides various professional strategies and literature-based resources to help improve the instructional process. An underlying theme throughout the chapter is that individuals who wish to enhance the process of helping adults learn can do so through their own initiatives.

Facilitating Adult Learning: A Transactional Process gives the reader a mechanism for understanding the dynamics and complexity of the teaching and learning encounter. It does not assume that the transactional process can be used in all adult learning educational settings. It does however challenge those interested in helping adults learn to discover greater understanding, excitement, and pleasure in facilitating adult learning.

Acknowledgments

In all projects such as this, various people play important roles to bring about its completion. This book is no exception. Special thanks to the people at Krieger Publishing Company, Robert Krieger, Mary Roberts, Marie Bowles, and all the support personnel, for making this book a reality. My sincere gratitude to my friends and colleagues who wrote chapters. Without all of you and the giving of your ideas and time this book would not have happened. To my graduate students I offer a debt of gratitude for the challenge you put forth and for the pleasure and opportunity of allowing me to be part of your learning experiences.

To T.J., my wife and best friend, a special thank you for the love, support, and meaningfulness you give to my life. It is with love that I dedicate this book to you. Lastly, a final farewell and thank you to Bo, my forever friend, for the gifts of the heart.

The Editor

Michael W. Galbraith is associate professor of adult education and coordinator of graduate studies in adult education at Temple University. He received his B.Ed. degree (1973) in social studies education and an M.Ed. degree (1981) in social foundations and gerontology from the University of Toledo, and his Ed.D. (1984) in adult education from Oklahoma State University.

Galbraith's main research and writing activities have focused on elder abuse, adult learning, professional certification, rural adult education, and community adult education. He has written numerous journal articles, book chapters, monographs, and several books including *Elder Abuse: Perspectives on an Emerging Crisis* (1986), *Professional Certification: Implications for Adult Education and HRD* (1986, with Jerry W. Gilley), *Adult Learning Methods: A Guide for Effective Instruction* (1990) and *Education Through Community Organizations* (1990). He is an active member in the Commission of Professors of Adult Education, American Association for Adult and Continuing Education, American Educational Research Association, and other state and regional adult education associations. He has held various voluntary leadership roles with adult education professional associations as well as serving on several editorial boards for professional journals.

Before coming to Temple University, Galbraith served on the faculties of the University of Missouri-Columbia and Oklahoma State University.

The Contributors

Paulette T. Beatty is associate professor of adult and interdisciplinary education at Texas A&M University.

Linda L. Benefield is a research associate at Texas A&M University.

Constance C. Blackwood is an educational specialist at the Idaho National Engineering Laboratory in Idaho Falls.

Ralph G. Brockett is associate professor of adult education at the University of Tennessee-Knoxville.

Stephen Brookfield is professor of higher and adult education at Teachers College, Columbia University.

Michael W. Galbraith is associate professor of adult education and coordinator of graduate studies in adult education at Temple University.

Roger Hiemstra is professor of adult education at Syracuse University.

Lani J. Linhart is a research associate at Texas A&M University.

Victoria J. Marsick is associate professor of adult and continuing education at Teachers College, Columbia University.

Burton Sisco is assistant professor of adult education at the University of Wyoming.

Karen E. Watkins is assistant professor of adult education and human resource development at the University of Texas at Austin.

Barbara A. White is an instructional development specialist for the Extension Service/Agricultural Experiment Station at Montana State University.

Bonnie S. Zelenak is director of the Learning Center and an assistant professor of adult education at the University of Missouri-Columbia.

CHAPTER 1

The Adult Learning Transactional Process

MICHAEL W. GALBRAITH

When facilitators and adult learners are engaged in an active, challenging, collaborative, critically reflective, and transforming educational encounter, a transactional process is occurring. Within this process learners are interacting with the facilitator and other learners, as well as with educational content, materials, ideas, values, and knowledge bases. The desired result, because of the interaction, is that all involved participants will think and act differently, whether it be about the personal, professional, political, social, or recreational aspects of their lives. Because of the complexity and multifaceted orientation of adult learners and the variety of settings in which the interaction occurs, there is no magic formula or guarantee that suggests each educational encounter will result in a rewarding and wholly meaningful teaching and learning transaction. As a result, adult learning becomes a challenging and creative activity demanding that facilitators and learners constantly reexamine their educational purposes, processes, values, needs, and desires in relationship to potential self-growth as well as to the enhancement of society. It is difficult to consider alternative ways of acting and thinking about held beliefs and values. However, this does not eliminate the obligation to scrutinize such actions and thoughts at the expense of potential growth and self-actualization.

Brookfield (1986) states that, "Simply because individuals who are chronologically adult are gathered together in a classroom does not mean that learning is automatically occurring" (p. 9). What is important to consider, according to Brookfield, "is the nature of the teaching-learning transaction itself and the extent to which features of mutual respect, negotiation, collaborativeness, and praxis are present" (p. 9). In other words, a transactional process must occur between those individuals involved in the educational activity before challenging, meaningful, and purposeful learning results. To enhance the likelihood that an effective teaching and learning transactional process will occur, the characteristics that comprise such a process must be understood as well as the central principles that guide effective practice. It is the focus of this chapter to examine the characteristics and principles that guide the adult learning transactional process.

CHARACTERISTICS OF THE TRANSACTIONAL PROCESS

The transactional process is a democratic and collaborative endeavor whereby facilitators and learners are engaged in a mutual act of challenge, critical reflection, sharing, support, and risk-taking. The essence of the transactional process is collaboration. Facilitators and learners are full partners in the learning experience. Brookfield (1986) suggests that "In an effective teaching-learning transaction all participants learn, no one member is regarded as having a monopoly on insight, and dissension and criticism are regarded as inevitable and desirable elements of the process" (p. 24). The importance of active and collaborative learning endeavors has been recognized throughout the years by others such as Dewey (1916), Lindeman (1926), Bryson (1936), Bergevin (1967), Rogers (1969), Freire (1970), Houle (1972), Kidd (1973), Knowles (1980), Knox, (1980, 1986), Brookfield (1986), Daloz (1986), Marsick (1987), and Galbraith (1990a). The transactional process is not a theory but a means by which facilitators and learners can make the experience a more meaningful, rewarding, and cooperative activity. The elements of the process however are constructed from adult learning theories that are based on adult characteristics, adult life situations, and changes in consciousness (Merriam, 1987).

Individuals engaged in a transactional process can enhance the endeavor by understanding the descriptive features of the process; the characteristics, roles, and skills of the facilitator; and the guiding principles.

Descriptive Features

Describing the most salient features of the transactional process is much easier than its implementation. When the vast array of settings in which adult learning occurs and the reasons for the learning, whether it be for personal, social, professional, recreational, or political, are considered it is rather naive to think that all elements of the transactional process that will be described will be incorporated. However, it does not eliminate our responsibility in the teaching and learning encounter to put forth the effort.

The most common elements of the transactional process are collaboration, support, respect, freedom, equality, critical reflection, critical analysis, challenge, and praxis. These features of the process hold true for both the facilitator and the adult learner who comprise the learning encounter. To incorporate these elements is to require facilitator and learner to scrutinize held values, beliefs, and ways of acting. Facilitators and learners must reconceptualize their roles, responsibilities, and purposes within the teaching and learning process. This process may even become painful because of the confrontation and challenge involved (Brookfield, 1987). The ultimate purpose, however, is not to create a threatening experience that becomes a block to learning but to collaborate through the educational experience to help participants each understand various aspects of their lives more fully.

The transactional process requires a certain type of discipline incorporating truth and responsibility, as well as an openness to challenge and risk taking. If we are to think and act differently as well as to engage in a healthy, meaningful educational transaction, we must be truthful. Peck states that "truth is reality . . . that which is false is unreal" (p. 44). The less clear we are about values, beliefs, and knowledge bases the less able we are to make wise decisions and to determine appropriate courses of action. Exploring the mystery of truth and reality demands an ongoing and constant refining and redefining.

Another element in the transactional process involves accepting responsibility for our actions and beliefs. Avoidance is less painful than confrontation. A transactional process demands that facilitators and learners accept the responsibilities of the roles, functions, and behaviors necessary to develop a collaborative and challenging learning encounter. Otherwise, if we attempt to give those responsibilities to some other individual or entity, we lose the free exchange of ideas, beliefs, and practices. As facilitators and adult learners we must be willing to accept appropriate responsibilities and have the capacity to reject responsibilities that are not truly ours.

An openness to challenge is also essential to the transactional process. A teaching and learning encounter dedicated to truth and responsibility is an educational situation characterized by a willingness to be challenged. The tendency to avoid challenge seems to be a characteristic of human nature. Therefore, challenge can be painful and at times seem unnatural. A collaborative and critically reflective learning experience must be a combination of contemplation and action. Freire (1970) calls this process praxis. Brookfield (1986) describes praxis as a process whereby:

> Learners and facilitators are involved in a continual process of activity, reflection upon activity, collaborative analysis of activity, new activity, further reflection and collaborative analysis, and so on. (p. 10)

To be successful in the process of praxis, an openness to challenge and a constant self-examination of beliefs and actions must be present. The challenge of examining the outside world is never as difficult as the examination of the world within. Probably because of the pain involved in the process of challenge and the need of self-examination for facilitators and learners alike, the majority shy away from it. The openness to challenge requires the act of giving something up, whether it is long-held beliefs, values, or actions, for the sake of personal growth. The balancing of those beliefs and actions that will be kept and those that will be foresaken gives us flexibility and the opportunity to think and act differently. Balancing involves an extension of the self rather than a sacrifice of the self. It involves an openness to change through the act of challenge.

Risk taking is another important feature of the transactional process for both the facilitator and the learner. Risk taking suggests that we enter new and unfamiliar territory, that we do things that we are unaccustomed to for the sake of change and personal growth. Risk taking involves courage. Peck (1979) suggests that courage "is not the absence of fear; it is the making of action in spite of fear, the moving out against the resistance engendered by fear into the unknown and into the future" (p. 131). In other words risk taking involves action.

A true adult learning transactional process engenders three types of risk taking: the risk of commitment, the risk of confrontation, and the risk of independence. A commitment to the ideals and actions of a transactional process is a risk. To submit to the transactional process suggests that facilitators and learners run the risk of self-confrontation and change. It involves the extension of oneself into new dimensions and territories of involvement and action. If adult learners are committed to a collaborative and challenging educational encounter, facilitators must be willing to make the same commitment—a commitment that suggests they too will experience opportunities for change, growth, and new learning.

The risk of confrontation is closely related to the openness to challenge held beliefs, values, and demonstrated actions. The purpose of confrontation is not to increase the amount of confusion in the learning experience but to enhance the amount of enlightenment. The act of confrontation should be an exercise in assisting adult learners to critically analyze why they think and act in the manner they do. It is helping them become aware of any incongruence in their feelings, attitudes, thoughts, and actions. Facilitators and adult learners should be each other's best critics. Confrontation and criticism should be sandwiched between caring and understanding. In addition, the risk of confrontation also involves wisdom—wisdom to know when to confront someone and whether or not they are ready for such confrontation and criticism.

The final risk that facilitators and adult learners are confronted with is the risk of independence. While this may seem rather odd, individuals engaged in a transactional process must take a leap toward self-direction and growth if meaningful learning is to occur (Brookfield, 1986; Knowles, 1980). However, not all who enter an educational activity are ready or at times willing to shed the psychological dependence they hold. Asking adult learners to take responsibility for their own learning as well as to seek individuality and independence can be a highly anxious and threatening experience. It would seem however that the highest form of meaningful learning is comprised of totally free choices and not acts of conformity and dependence on others. With the most salient features of a transactional process being collaboration and challenge, individuals who are not willing to take the risk of independence would not experience the pleasure of intellectual growth, freedom and the excitement of exploring new dimensions of thinking and acting.

The descriptive features and elements of the adult learning transactional process can be recognized in the adult education literature (e.g., Brookfield, 1986, 1987; Knowles, 1980; Knox, 1986; Marsick, 1987, 1988; Mezirow, 1981, 1985; Schön, 1983, 1987). While not all aspects of their work follow the same process for bringing about an effective and meaningful teaching and learning transaction, the notion of a learner-centered approach that incorporates the elements of a democratic process that allows the free exchange of ideas, beliefs, and practices is present. Brookfield's (1986) work seems to capture the essence of the descriptive features presented thus far. For the present only the principles of effective practice developed by Brookfield (1986) will be described in relationship to the transactional process.

The first principle of effective practice according to Brookfield (1986) is that adults participate in learning as a result of their own volition. Because participation is voluntary, adult learners must realize the benefit of their participation or they will withdraw from the activity. In the transactional process, an understanding of the uniqueness of adult learners is essential if a meaningful educational encounter is to be realized. Part of that understanding is the realization that adult learners have the freedom to voluntarily choose in what learning they will participate.

To be engaged in an effective transactional process, facilitators and learners must demonstrate in their behavior toward one another a sense of caring, support, respect, and truthfulness. Brookfield's second principle of effective practice also suggests that all participants must respect each other's self-worth. He writes, "To behave in a manner disrespectful to others, to denigrate their contributions, or to embarrass them publicly through extended attention to their apparent failings are behaviors that are, in educational terms, disastrous" (Brookfield, 1986, p. 13). Although challenge is an important element in the process, this does not mean it is conducted through intimidation and disrespect. Establishing a conducive social and psychological climate for learning early in the educational process assists participants in understanding each other's uniqueness, individuality, and self-worth, thus allowing challenge, criticism, and a free exchange of ideas.

The third principle of effective practice suggested by Brookfield is the existence of a collaborative and participatory component in the educational activity. Collaboration is perhaps the foremost essential feature of the transactional process. All participants should be engaged in assessing needs, setting objectives, selecting appropriate methodologies and materials, and developing evaluation procedures as well as actively participating in the facilitation of the learning.

Brookfield's next two principles of effective practice, praxis and critical reflection, can also be identified in the transactional process through the descriptive features of contemplation and action, risk taking, confrontation, and challenge. Praxis and critical reflection seem to constitute some similar elements concerned with critical analysis development that leads to different way of thinking and acting. Praxis, however, cannot result without critical reflectivity.

It would seem rather foolish to accept these principles of effective practice and not assume that the consequence of such practice would be assisting participants to be self-directed in their educational endeavors, which is Brookfield's last principle. The principles of understanding and respecting the self-worth of adult learners, collaboration, praxis, and critical reflection lead to self-direction and empowerment. The essence of the transactional process is to move adult learners toward independence and responsibility for their own learning and subsequent actions.

All these interrelated elements can be incorporated into a set of principles that lead to effective practice. The facilitator is a major player in the success of the process and requires certain characteristics, roles, and skills.

Facilitator Characteristics, Roles, and Skills

Characteristics. Numerous practical resource books can assist the facilitator to be more effective in the process of helping adults learn (Bergevin, Morris & Smith, 1963; Brookfield, 1986; Daloz, 1986; Dickinson, 1973; Draves, 1984; Galbraith, 1990b; Hayes, 1989; Knowles, 1980; Knox, 1980, 1986; Robinson, 1979; Rosenblum, 1985; Seaman & Fellenz, 1989). Because the transactional process suggests that the educational encounter must be collaborative and challenging, the facilitator must be proficient in content area, understanding adult learners, and adult learning methodologies as well as possess personality characteristics and interpersonal skills that engender an image of caring, trust, and encouragement. Knox (1980) states that facilitators through their personality should suggest a sense of self-confidence, informality, enthusiasm, responsiveness, and creativity.

Apps (1981) provides a list of characteristics appropriate to the transactional process such as showing an interest in the learner, possessing a good personality, showing an interest in the subject matter, and demonstrating objectivity in presenting the subject matter and in dealing with learners. Such characteristics suggest that facilitators are more concerned about learners than about things and events, are able to relate theory to practice, are open to a variety of instructional strategies and approaches, are encouraging and challenging, and are capable of creating a positive psychological learning environment. Draves (1984) writes that facilitators of adult learning must have understanding, flexibility, patience, humor, practicality, creativity, and preparation. Tough (1979) suggests that ideal helpers are warm, loving, caring, and accepting of learners, have a high regard for the learner's self-planning abilities, view themselves as participating in a dialogue between equals with learners, and are open to change and new experiences. Caring, listening, and passion are powerful elements as well as the capacity to provide emotional support when it is needed.

Roles. The facilitator's roles are diverse because of the multifaceted nature of adult learning and the settings in which it occurs. Within a transactional process and the context of the learning and its outcomes, the facilitator may be the challenger, role model, mentor, coach, demonstrator, content resource person, and learning guide. The learning process is a collaborative and challenging encounter that incorporates diverse characteristics and strategies. A learner-centered approach implies that we have relinquished the idea of totally controlling the teaching and learning situation. We have moved in the direction of collaboration in an effort to assist learners to become critically reflective and independent individuals who are aware of and understand the nature of their beliefs, values, and actions.

Skills. Facilitators can not expect a meaningful educational encounter if they do not possess certain skills that can be translated into effective practice. In the transactional process, helping skills, motivational strategy skills, and instructional planning skills are essential.

Brockett (1983) examined counseling and helping skill approaches and related them to the process of helping adults learn. Based on the work of Egan (1975), such skills as attending, responding, and understanding were identified as basic components. Attending is a situation that suggests the caring, observing, and listening presence of the helper toward the learner. It involves the physical and psychological dimensions of being with another person. Brockett writes that "by attending to the words and actions of the learner, a facilitator can begin to build a foundation upon which a productive relationship may be established" (p. 9). The second helping skill is that of responding. Responding means to help learners explore their behaviors. Within this approach, the facilitator must demonstrate empathy toward understanding the learner's world, respect the individual's self-worth and uniqueness, demonstrate sincerity and genuineness, and provide encouragement. Through the concept of responding, facilitators can provide a challenging and risk-taking environment for learners to freely and openly explore their needs, values, beliefs, and actions. Attending and responding help establish the psychological climate as well as rapport with the learners. The third helping skill is that of understanding, which is a process of discerning the issue and providing assistance toward some resolution. It means collaboratively mapping out options and strategies with the learner who in return can implement some course of inquiry toward resolution.

It is obvious from the approaches mentioned above that the facilitator of adult learning takes on the role of counselor in the transactional process. The implementation of the helping process cannot be accomplished without possessing good communication skills. Bateson (1972) and Egan (1986) suggest that at the core of effective interpersonal relations is open and honest communication between all involved individuals. It is inappropriate to confront learners with a double message where one message denies the other. Such a situation leaves the learner unable either to comment on the messages being expressed or to correct any discrimination regarding which message to respond to (Bateson 1972). Attending, responding, and understanding all involve communication between facilitator and learner. It is essential in the transactional process that thoughtful, open, and sincere dialogue exists. Communicating effectively demands that we understand adult learners and their present intellectual and psychological dimensions. Without this understanding, our communication with learners will be meaningless and void of any evidence that we seek a collaborative educational encounter.

Another essential skill for the facilitator of the transactional process is that of establishing strategies that motivate the learner to

engage in meaningful, collaborative, challenging, and critically reflective learning. Facilitators can help establish a learning setting
that encourages adult learners to be motivated toward wanting to
think and act differently. Primary attention should be given to
Wlodkowski (1985, 1990) who provides a useful set of motivational strategies that relate to such areas as attitudes, needs, stimulation, affect, competence, and reinforcement. The format used by
Wlodkowski (1985) describes goals and the specific strategy to help
reach each goal. Sixty-eight strategies help facilitators to:

- Help learners create a positive attitude toward the subject and
  learning situation.

- Develop a positive learner self-concept for learning.

- Establish learner expectancy for success.

- Ensure responsiveness to learner needs.

- Build learner interest.

- Develop learner involvement.

- Encourage and integrate learner emotions within the learning
  process.

- Increase learner awareness of progress, mastery, achievement,
  and responsibility in learning.

- Help learners to be aware of positive changes their learning has
  produced.

In a collaborative, challenging, and reflective transactional
process, facilitators can use various motivational strategies suggested by Brophy (1983, 1987), Deci and Ryan (1985), Kanfer and
Goldstein (1986), Keller (1987), and Wlodkowski (1985, 1990).
For example, in dealing with creating a positive attitude and learning climate, you could share something about yourself as well as
have the learners each introduce themselves and share some general
information about why they are participating, what they want from
the educational encounter, and how their experiences add to the
situation (Wlodkowski, 1985). You can share how the learners'
cooperation and collaboration will assist in the design, planning,

and evaluation of the course of study. Provide opportunities to respond to any concerns about the expectations. Another useful strategy is to provide opportunities to select topics, projects, and assignments that will also allow the use of various learning methods. Facilitators can offer challenges that learners can apply to their personal, social and professional lives. Additional strategies are constant feedback regarding the learners' progress as well as encouragement and critical confrontation related to their learning. It is out of the scope of this chapter to present specific motivational strategies for each type of learning situation. However, it is imperative to realize that as the stage is set for a transactional process it is essential to incorporate the elements of effective practice.

Helping skills, communication skills, and motivational strategy skills are all important in the development of an effective transactional process, but they are not enough. Facilitators must also possess skills in instructional planning (Galbraith, 1989).

Components of Instructional Planning

Instructional planning is comprised of needs assessment, context analysis, setting learning objectives, organizing learning activities, selecting learning methods, and evaluation. Each component and its various subcomponents can be initiated through the collaborative approach with facilitator and learner sharing equal responsibility. However, as Brookfield (1986) suggests:

> Facilitators have to be as wary of supporting every inclination, preference, or demand of learners as they are of forcing these same learners to follow a lockstep sequence of previously prescribed educational activities. In both instances learners are liable to develop an uncritical stance toward their own personal and intellectual development; in the one case because their opinion is never challenged or questioned, in the other because they are given no choice or chance to voice an opinion. Either option denies the essentially transactional nature of teaching-learning. . . . (p. 146)

The facilitator and learner have essential roles and responsibilities within the instructional planning process. This does not mean, however, that the instructional planning process is wholly nondirective and that facilitators abdicate their responsibilities and ignore their experience and expertise in helping adults learn. A detailed examination of the process is out of the scope of this chapter; however, a cursory review of the instructional planning process will be presented here.

Needs Assessment. A needs assessment should identify the gaps between the learner's current and desired proficiencies as perceived by the learner and others. The assessment of needs should be ongoing throughout the planning process in an effort to ensure that individual and program desired outcomes are congruent.

There is no consensus on the most appropriate method for identifying learner needs. Each selected method will generate different types of information depending who is involved in the assessment. If you as a facilitator make the assessment, the current proficiency level will be identified and compared against the standards desired by you. If the learners themselves are the source of identifying needs, the results will most likely reveal information about "their preferences for the topics they want to study and the proficiencies they want to enhance and about the choices they make when given opportunities to participate in educative activities" (Knox, 1986, p. 57.). Needs identified by learners and by facilitators can be distinguished as felt needs (wants, desires, wishes) which relate to the learner and prescribed needs which relate to the skills, knowledge, behaviors, and values that facilitators feel adults should acquire (Brookfield, 1986). Combining felt needs and prescribed needs is a more rationale approach in the identification of learner needs and desired outcomes. In approaching needs assessment in this manner, a mutual collaborative environment can result that ensures greater participation and a desire to persist and achieve in the educational encounter.

Highly informal and intuitive to highly formal and in-depth analysis techniques can be used in the needs assessment activity (Cameron, 1988; Knox, 1986; Zemke & Kramlinger, 1982). You can use data-collection procedures such as individual interviews, questionnaires, tests, observation checklists, self-assessment diagnostic instruments, surveys, and performance analysis techniques. Various strengths and weaknesses are associated with each type of procedure. In terms of the collaborative spirit, the importance of the needs identified tend to be judged "in light of expectations of learners, yourself, and representatives of organizations" (Knox, 1986, p. 62).

Context Analysis. Context analysis is another component in the instructional planning process. It considers the societal trends and issues, the resources, and the mission of the provider organization and how it influences the transactional process. By combining the data of the various influences with information found through the needs assessment process, feasible learning objectives can be agreed upon by facilitator and learners. Context analysis is concerned with the influences on the setting in which the learning occurs as well as where the learners are likely to apply their knowledge. It is important to understand the impact of these influences on the learners and on the instructional process. Analysis of current issues, trends, technologies, and so forth can suggest the effects they have on the personal and sociopolitical aspects of the learners' lives. The contextual influences affect the decisions facilitators can make within the instructional process, curricula, program formats, and evaluative standards.

Setting Learning Objectives. Another component in the instructional planning process is setting learning objectives. An objective is the intended or desired outcome and proficiency level that the learner should obtain as a result of participating in the educational experience. Objectives may focus on knowledge, skill, or attitude enhancement or a combination of the three to reach the desired outcomes. Setting objectives should be the joint responsibility of you and the learners who will participate in the educational encounter. Selecting and setting learning objectives should draw heavily from the needs assessment and context analysis information. Setting educational objectives should be an ongoing and interactive process, introduced during the planning stages and conducted throughout the implementation of the educational activity. By utilizing a collaborative approach on agreeing to the learning objectives, adult learners can increase their understanding of and commitment to achieving the objectives, understand the relationship between current and desired proficiencies, reflect on questions that need addressing, and acquire a framework for learning how to learn beyond the present educational activity (Knox, 1980; Smith, 1982). You can use the agreed upon objectives to assist in the process of selecting materials, outlining content, deciding on methods of teaching and learning, and preparing evaluation procedures (Knox, 1986).

It is impossible to identify through prespecified objectives all the unplanned and unanticipated learning needs of the adult learner, therefore opportunities to modify the educational objectives must be present as the educational encounter unfolds. Brookfield (1986) writes that:

> the most fundamental flaw with the predetermined objectives approach . . . is its tendency to equate one form of adult learning—instrumental learning (how to perform technical or psychomotor operations more effectively)—with the sum total of adult learning. It neglects completely the domain of the most significant personal learning—the kind that results from reflection on experiences and from trying to make sense of one's life by exploring the meanings others have assigned to similar experiences. (p. 213)

Adult learners develop differently throughout and because of their educational experiences, and as a result the identified learning objectives should not be considered unchanging and unchallengeable but should seek to correspond to such developmental change.

Organizing Learning Activities. Organizing learning activities is another component in planning. Information and decisions that were made from the needs assessment, context analysis, and objective setting activities transfer into intended outcomes for the educational activity. With the involvement of the learners, you can select and organize learning activities that will meet those outcomes. Conversely, selecting the most appropriate learning activities should also depend upon the desired outcomes such as knowledge acquisition, practice, application, and so forth. It is important to understand the current proficiency level and the preferred learning styles of the learners, which can be accomplished, for example, through competency lists and self-diagnostic inventories and by asking how they like to process information and what methods they like to use in that process (Galbraith, 1987).

Selecting Learning Methods. Selecting the most appropriate instructional and learning methods is another important component if an effective transactional process is to occur. A litany of methodologies exists and each one is influenced by the content, the learning objectives, the desired outcomes, the characteristics of the learners, the size of the group, and the availability of time, equipment, facilities, and budget (Galbraith, 1990b; Klevins, 1987; Knox, 1986; Seaman & Fellenz, 1989). Elsewhere in this book an examination of the most salient methods and techniques that can be used in the transactional process will be made. Related to the selection of methods is the selection and preparation of instructional materials to use in the identified learning activities. The primary criteria for selecting materials, whether they be by you or the learner, should be the educational purposes they serve in conjunction with the learning needs and learning styles. An array of materials exists such as books, programmed texts, radio audiotapes, slides, charts, photographs, slide tapes, television, computer software, case studies, and other simulations such as critical incident cases, and discussion guides (Knox, 1986). Selection criteria include how the selected materials assist in meeting the learning objectives, and how appropriate and responsive they are to the learner's background, current level of proficiency, and motivation (Wilson, 1983).

Evaluation. Evaluation is the final component of the instructional planning process. You are one of the main users of the evaluation data; therefore, such findings can aid in your own improvement as a facilitator of adult learning. Evaluative procedures can help determine if the participants in the learning activity reached their learning objectives and desired outcomes. In addition, some of the unplanned results and incidental outcomes of the learning encounter can also be determined (Scriven, 1972). In the spirit of the transactional process, adult learners in the program must be actively involved in a participatory evaluation process. A learner-centered approach may use a number of evaluative strategies such as critierion-referenced evaluation (Knowles, 1980), naturalistic evaluation (Lincoln & Guba, 1985), participatory evaluation (Brookfield, 1986), or an andragogical and collaborative mode of evaluation (Deshler, 1984). Using these or an adaptation of the most salient components and features of a number of evaluative procedures to bring about a collaborative and participatory effort is paramount in the transactional process. A more in-depth examination of the evaluation process will be made elsewhere in this book. For now, it is important to recognize that within the transactional process evaluation is an essential component as well as an essential skill for the facilitator.

The essence of the transactional process is not new. Through recent years the importance of how we can work more effectively with adult learners has captured the attention of various educators (Brookfield, 1986; Cross, 1981; Galbraith, 1989, 1990a; Knowles, 1980; Knox, 1986; Marsick, 1987; Mezirow, 1981, 1985; Schön,

1987; Wildemeersch & Leirman, 1988). In accepting the described characteristics, the various roles, and the skills essential for the facilitator within the transactional process, Cassivi (1989) suggests that we are maintaining a legacy in the education of adults that has stood firm through the ages.

GUIDING PRINCIPLES OF THE TRANSACTIONAL PROCESS

The principles that guide the transactional process apply to the teaching and learning encounter and to the way learning activities are designed and implemented. To have an effective transactional process, the following six principles should be present:

1. An appropriate philosophical orientation must guide the educational encounter.

2. The diversity of adult learners must be recognized and understood.

3. A conducive psychosocial climate for learning must be created.

4. Challenging teaching and learning interactions must occur.

5. Critical reflection and praxis must be fostered.

6. Independence must be encouraged.

Because of the multifaceted nature of adult learning and the settings in which it occurrs, not all of these six principles may be easily implemented or observed in all educational encounters. However, to begin to realize an effective adult learning transactional process, incorporate the identified principles, at least in some degree. These guiding principles have numerous implications within the process of helping adults learn, examine, change, and interpret the many dimensions and facets of their lives. What follows is an examination of each principle in greater detail.

Maintain a Philosophy

Elias and Merriam (1980) write that "philosophy raises questions about what we do and why we do it" (p. 5). They continue by stating that a:

philosophy of adult education does not equip a person with knowledge about what to teach, how to teach, or how to organize a program. It is more concerned with the why of education and with the logical analysis of the various elements of the educational process. (p. 8)

In addition, philosophy will help focus on the ethical issues associated with the relationship of adult learning facilitation and adult learning as well as with other major dimensions of practice (Brockett, 1988; Sork, 1987). No shortage exists in the literature as related to philosophy of adult education and the various frameworks of thought (Apps, 1973, 1976; Bergevin, 1967; Elias & Merriam, 1980; Hiemstra, 1988; Lindeman, 1926; McKenzie, 1985; Merriam, 1982, 1984a; Podeschi, 1986; Zinn, 1983, 1990).

The assumptions made about the transactional process, its characteristics, and the roles of the facilitator and learner suggest that components of progressive, humanistic, and radical philosophies are the most appropriate frameworks in which to guide the educational encounter. Each of the three philosophies is consistent with the components of the transactional process: collaborating; stimulating critical reflection; and promoting intellectual, personal, professional, practical, social, political, and economic growth through the act of challenge. Learners are viewed as partners in the educational encounter who assume responsibility for their own behavior and learning. Facilitators of adult learning serve as guides, mentors, helpers, and partners in the learning process. Those who accept the progressive, humanistic, and radical philosophies believe in using methods that involve problem solving, group discussion, collaborative instruction, and self-discovery that lead to the enhancement of self-direction and independence. They understand that participation in learning is voluntary and the decision rests with the learner.

Through understanding the framework for each philosophy and its beliefs, you are better able to reflect critically on your professional practice and how it is influenced. A useful self-administering, self-scoring, and self-interpreting instrument entitled *Philosophy of Adult Education Inventory* developed by Zinn (1983, 1990) can assist you in identifying your philosophical orientation. Elias and Merriam (1980) provide an excellent overview and a helpful way of organizing and understanding philosophical frameworks about adult education. A personal philosophy worksheet developed by

Hiemstra (1988) can also serve as a tool for working through personal values and beliefs and relating them to professional practice. Although not an inventory that identifies your philosophy orientation, the *Principles of Adult Learning Scale* (PALS) designed by Conti (1985, 1990) can identify your teaching behavior mode (teacher-directed or collaborative). By comparing your teaching mode discovered through PALS to the philosophical orientation found in Zinn's philosophy inventory, you can determine if your facilitation practices are consistent with your philosophical beliefs and values as they relate to the educational encounter.

Through the various resources cited above, you can identify a philosophical framework that makes you aware of what you are doing and why you are doing it. Practice must be guided by a philosophical orientation consistent with the essential characteristics of the transactional process.

Understand the Adult Learner

Facilitators in a transactional process understand the diversity and variability of adult learners. It is the multifaceted physiological, psychological, sociological, and developmental aspects of the adult learner that contribute to and make a challenging and enriching educational encounter. The various dimensions or characteristics of the adult learner are interrelated, thus one dimension of the individual is affected by every other dimension (Cross, 1981; Daloz, 1986; Jarvis, 1987; Knox, 1986; Krupp, 1982; Long, 1983, 1990). Krupp (1982) suggests that understanding this multifaceted characterization is to understand the adult learner from a holistic perspective. This seems most appropriate, especially when working with adults who have diverse reasons for participating, are at various stages in their adult development, and who possess a multitude of learning styles.

Boshier and Collins (1985) identified multiple reasons for participating in educational activities and clustered them into six categories: cognitive interest, social stimulation, social contact, external expectations, community service, and professional advancement. Understanding the reasons for adult participation and remembering that in most learning encounters such participation is voluntary, facilitators have the challenge of using such information for building more rewarding and persistent learning situations. They seek to develop collaborative, challenging, critically reflective, and transforming encounters where the adult learner is the user of the education instead of just the recipient. Participation information becomes a tool in developing responsive educational encounters. Facilitators create appropriate learning opportunities, materials, techniques, and strategies that encourage learners to search for a higher level of understanding as well as alternative ways of thinking and acting.

Another important component in understanding the adult learner is to recognize the multifaceted aspects of adult development and the implications for the transactional process. Adult learners are varied in their physical, social, psychological, ego, moral, and learning developmental directions (Daloz, 1986; Knox, 1977; Merriam, 1984b). Each learner who enters the educational encounter has experienced different marker events, transitions, roles, and crises. Such experiences provide a fertile opportunity for reappraisal and exploration of ideas and actions (Hughes, Graham, & Galbraith, 1986). Facilitators have an opportunity to assist learners in developing learning strategies and activities that fit their diverse backgrounds and interests. This active involvement helps learners assume responsibility for their own learning as well as bolster their capabilities to be independent in other facets of their personal, professional, social, and recreational lives. Understanding adult development also provides to the transactional process the characterization that each individual is unique, separate, and deserving of respect (Brookfield, 1986).

Another dimension to understanding the diversity of the adult learner is to recognize the various learning styles that each individual brings to the educational encounter. Learning styles are the ways that individuals prefer to engage and process information in learning activities. Adult development dimensions influence learning ability and style throughout the various stages of life. Numerous literature sources are available for the facilitator to investigate the diverse learning style information and inventories (Bonham, 1988; Claxton & Murrell, 1987; Cornett, 1983; Dixon, 1985; Galbraith, 1987; Galbraith & Sanders, 1987; James & Galbraith, 1985; Kolb, 1984; Price, 1983; Smith, 1982). Some of the inventories view learning style from a cognitive perspective while others view it from an affective or physiological perspective. No universal prescription concerning the most salient style can be made, especially when the multifaceted nature of adult learners is considered. The important point is to recognize the diversity of adult learners and their styles and to utilize diverse learning methods that best fit a collaborative, challenging, and critically reflective educational encounter (Galbraith, 1990b; Knox, 1986; Lewis, 1986). Using experiential techniques such as simulations, role plays, case studies, critical incidents, and inquiry teams allows adult learners to filter their perceptions through their own experiences, needs, and developmental changes. Other methods and techniques appropriate for the transactional process will be discussed in another chapter.

Understanding the diversity and variability of the adult learner is vital to the transactional process. It assists the facilitator and learner to evolve from unquestioning conformity in the learning situation to one of collaboration, reappraisal and exploration, and praxis.

Create a Conducive Psychosocial Climate

There are various components or variables that contribute to the environmental climate of an educational encounter. Physical environment, which is one major component, is concerned with ergonomics—the interactions of people with their physical and spatial environments. Some of the elements for consideration would be the arrangement of classroom seating as well as building characteristics such as lighting, ventilation, colorful decor, appropriate temperature settings, and refreshment areas (Ennis et al., 1989; Knowles and Associates, 1984; Lean, 1984; Vosko, 1984). The physical climate is important in the creation of a conducive learning environment; however, in most cases it is not something you have a great deal of control over. What seems to be most important within the transactional process is the development of a conducive psychosocial climate. This you can control.

The psychosocial climate is concerned with the psychological aspects as well as the cultural dimensions of the educational encounter. This includes the relationship among the learners, rapport and communication, opportunity for participation, values and belief systems which hold meaning for learners, expectations, and clarity of goals (Knowles and Associates, 1984; Tagiuri, 1968). If an effective transactional process is to occur, a climate that suggests mutual respect, collaborativeness, mutual trust, supportiveness, openness to challenge and criticism, risk taking, pleasure, and friendliness must be present. Establishing this begins with the very first encounter you have with the adult learners. Introduce yourself in a manner that relates your philosophical orientation, your self-image, their abilities as learners, and the mutuality, encouragement, and support that will take place within the educational encounter. Getting the participants involved immediately through introductory activities that provide personal and professional information is helpful. Such activities help everyone get acquainted and also create opportunities for informal conversations among the learners. Brue (1985) suggests that "ice-breakers" can be very effective in developing a nonthreatening, nondefensive environment and at the same time provide to the entire group a common experience that will lead into the educational activities.

A conducive psychosocial climate can be maintained throughout the planning process of assessing learning needs, establishing learning activities, and developing evaluation strategies. Utilizing collaborative and challenging approaches that accept the learners' input tells participants that they are important in the development of the educational encounter and that their perceptions and contributions matter (Schlossberg, Lynch, & Chickering, 1989). You can challenge, in ways that are nonthreatening or personally disturbing, the learners and learners can challenge you and each other. A positive psychosocial climate not only invites learners to be collaborative and challenging but also provides an occasion for them to explore their creativity (Patterson, 1986).

Provide Challenging Interactions

In a transactional process you are asking learners to engage in an educational encounter that involves them in questioning their held judgments, actions, and assumptions. You are asking them to confront, scrutinize, and question the way they think and act. This important task can begin through the process of challenge. Working toward this process has already begun if the appropriate philosophical orientation has been established, the diversity of adult learners is understood, and if a conducive psychosocial climate has been created. Challenge and confrontation should be viewed as a natural progression and component within the transactional process. However, "the right to challenge someone must be earned. . . . [and]. . . . when helpers' actions contradict their declared beliefs and intentions, they have forfeited their right to challenge" (Brookfield, 1987, p. 91).

Providing challenging interactions should have as its primary purpose the promotion of development of learners who can think critically and reflectively. Challenge is the last most single essential component necessary before an individual can develop alternative ways of thinking and acting (Egan, 1986). It begins with taking a stance of caring, attending, and listening to the learner while all along understanding how much the learner can emotionally take before such challenge becomes personally disturbing and threatening. Appropriate challenges are those that call out for closure, while at the same time provide insight to how this new knowledge can be applied to the learners' lives. As Daloz (1986) suggests, you should provide a "mirror" for learners which allows them to see themselves in a different way, to see how they have changed and developed as a result of their accomplishments through the process of challenge. Various strategies will provide appropriate challenge to the learners while assisting them in questioning givens and examining the assumptions that form the foundation of their thoughts and actions. Such strategies may include peer learning groups, critical questioning, critical incident exercises, role playing, and crisis-decision simulations.

An effective transactional process incorporates the process of challenge. It suggests that challenging one another is an appropriate component within the educational encounter and that learning is not an unquestioning process. Challenging interactions provide both facilitator and learner with an opportunity to scrutinize thoughts and actions. This hopefully fosters critical reflection and praxis, which is the next principle within the transactional process.

Foster Critical Reflection and Praxis

Fostering critical reflection and praxis is paramount in the transactional process. Learning is comprised of both psychological and social constructs, therefore when you encourage learners to examine and understand the nature of their knowledge, values, assumptions, ideologies, judgments, and behaviors in a broader context, you are helping them to be critically reflective as well as fostering a sense of how all this is culturally and socially constructed (Brookfield, 1986; Jarvis, 1987; Marsick, 1987). Within the process of critical reflection, learners begin to question how their assumptions and behaviors, for example, affect the various aspects of their personal, professional, and political lives. Mezirow (1985) states that critical reflectivity is "the bringing of one's assumptions, premises, criteria, and schemata into consciousness and vigorously critiquing them" (p. 25). Critical reflection is a knowing act that fosters in learners a questioning and critically aware frame of mind. Within such a process you are asking learners to take risks and challenges. They must go beneath the surface and think about the underlying assumptions, values, and behaviors as well as the consequences and relationship to their lives in some broader context. Critical reflectivity brings about a transformation in learning that has incorporated the elements of freedom, valid reasoning, openness, mutuality, collaboration, and critical discourse (Mezirow and Associates, 1990). It should result in intellectual and critical development which is transformed into an observable and for some an unobservable activity. This process is known as praxis.

Brookfield (1986) suggests that "praxis is placed at the heart of good facilitation" (p. 10). He writes that this process:

> centers on the need for educational activity to engage the learner in a continuous and alternating process of investigation and exploration, followed by action grounded in this exploration, followed by reflection on this action, followed by further investigation and exploration, followed by further action, and so on. (p. 15)

This continual process of reflectivity and activity takes place "within the context of learners' past, current, and future experiences" (p. 15). As mentioned above, some of the actions may be observable while others may be unobservable or cognitive in nature. Throughout this process of reflection and action, experimenting with and reshaping of thoughts and activities occur in relationship to the learners' experiences. Schön (1987) refers to this as "reflection-in-action" and suggests that such a process "serves to reshape what we are doing while we are doing it" (p. 26). Utilizing strategies and techniques such as critical questioning, critical incident exercises, mentoring, coaching, practicums, role playing, debates, critical analysis, modeling, and case studies can begin to provide valuable approaches to bridging the gap between the processes of critical reflection and praxis.

The primary consequence of fostering critical reflection and praxis within the transactional process is that it promotes the development of critical thinkers who can identify and explore assumptions under which they think and act. Brookfield (1987) writes that critical thinkers understand the importance of identifying and challenging those assumptions, as well as imagining and exploring alternative ways of thinking and acting—which leads to reflective skepticism. Hopefully, such exploration helps learners to interpret and question beliefs and actions from new viewpoints in relationship to the various aspects of their lives.

Within the transactional process, if critical reflection and praxis are encouraged, you and the learners will develop a better framework for thinking and acting. Ultimately, this is translated into more meaningful and effective practice as detailed in such works by Brookfield (1986, 1987), Cervero (1988), Jarvis (1987), Knox (1986), Marsick (1987), and Schön (1983, 1987).

Encourage Independence

Considering the five principles discussed thus far, it is not surprising that the final principle deals with encouraging independence within the educational encounter. When you incorporate an appropriate philosophical orientation, collaboration, a conducive psychosocial climate, challenge, critical reflection and praxis into the transactional process, you are ultimately asking learners to become engaged in transformative learning that leads to independence, autonomy, empowerment, and self-direction (Mezirow, 1985). Encouraging independence suggests that learners should question and scrutinize held values, ideologies, and behaviors and regard this newfound knowledge as relative and contextual. Independence allows learners to reinterpret, renegotiate, and recreate their perspectives which results in alternative ways of thinking and acting (Brookfield, 1986). It gives them an awareness of their learning processes and the recognition of any self-imposed limits.

This principle states that the facilitator should encourage independence. However, it has been this writer's experience that not all learners welcome the opportunity and responsibility for their own learning. Therefore, as a facilitator you must help guide those individuals from the state of dependence to some degree of independence and self-direction in their learning and educational activities. External sources or stimuli play an important part in the movement to independence. You must at times "present learners with alternatives to their current ways of thinking, behaving, and living" (Brookfield, 1986, p. 19). Through this process you are assisting learners to consciously question and scrutinize their intellectual ideologies, which must be an internal process. The movement toward independence involves the facilitator and the learner. It is the combination of the external activities with the internal dispositions. Independence helps develop self-directed learners who are aware of the contextuality and cultural constructs that influence their thoughts and actions. Encouraging independence allows learners to explore and recognize their own self-directedness.

Knowles (1975), Tough (1979), and others suggest that self-directed learning is a process whereby learners are capable of identifying learning objectives, diagnosing needs, recognizing appropriate resources and strategies, and evaluating the learning experience. However, viewing self-directed learning in this manner only accounts for the external management of the educational encounter and does not address the internal and critical reflective dimensions of the learning. Brookfield (1986) writes that "Self-directed learning as the mode of learning characteristic of an adult who is in the process of realizing his or her adulthood is concerned as much with an internal change of consciousness as with the external management of instructional events" (p. 58). Because of the multifaceted aspects of learning situations and the nature of adult learners, how fast one moves from the state of dependence to self-directedness and independence may depend upon the individual and the situation (Brockett & Hiemstra, 1985). Investigating the works of Brookfield (1984, 1985, 1986), Caffarella and O'Donnell (1987), Long and Associates (1988), Mezirow (1985), and Spear and Mocker (1984) can help clarify the complexity of self-directed learning as it relates to the external and internal dimensions associated with adult learning.

Encouraging adult learners to seek independence in their learning activities is asking them to explore alternatives to their assumptions, beliefs, values, ideologies, and actions. Hopefully, these alternatives will enhance the sense of independence that leads to a continuous transformation of thinking and acting. As a facilitator, you can encourage independence within the transactional process by suggesting techniques that allow creativity and thoughtful contemplation. Various strategies for assisting in this are detailed in other chapters within this book.

CONCLUSION

When you engage in an educational encounter, the psychological and social dimensions of the teaching and learning process mesh to create a dynamic process. To the enhancement of this dynamic process, collaboration, challenge, critical reflection, and praxis are incorporated to bring about what has been described as a transactional process. Within this process, involved individuals examine held assumptions and perspectives about the way they think and act. Through the transactional process adult learners are encouraged to seek alternative interpretations of their thoughts and actions and to understand the contextuality and relativity of them. This chapter has presented six principles that guide the transactional process and the role that each particular principle plays to bring about a more effective and meaningful teaching and learning transaction. The transactional process provides a mechanism for you and adult learners who are engaged in an educational encounter to seek out and find greater understanding and meaning in your formal and informal learning experiences through active discovery and exploration.

REFERENCES

Apps, J. W. (1973). *Toward a working philosophy of adult education*. Syracuse: Syracuse University Publications in Continuing Education.

Apps, J. W. (1976). A foundation for action. In C. Klevins (Ed.), *Materials and methods in continuing education* (pp. 18–26). Los Angeles: Klevens.

Apps, J. W. (1981). *The adult learner on campus: A guide for instructors and administrators*. Chicago: Follett.

Bateson, G. (1972). *Steps to an ecology of mind*. New York: Ballantine Books.

Bergevin, P. (1967). *A philosophy for adult education*. New York: Seabury.

Bergevin, P., Morris, D., & Smith, R. (1963). *Adult education procedures: A handbook of tested patterns for effective participation*. New York: Seabury.

Bonham, L. (1988). Learning style use: In need of perspective. *Lifelong Learning: An Omnibus of Practice and Research, 11*(5), 14–17, 19.

Boshier, R., & Collins, J. (1985). The Houle typology after twenty-two years: A large-scale empirical test. *Adult Education Quarterly, 35*(3), 113–130.

Brockett, R. (1983). Facilitator roles and skills. *Lifelong Learning: The Adult Years, 6*(5), 7–9.

Brockett, R. (Ed.). (1988). *Ethical issues in adult education.* New York: Teachers College Press.

Brockett, R., & Hiemstra, R. (1985). Bridging the theory-practice gap in self-directed learning. In S. Brookfield (Ed.), *Self-directed learning: From theory to practice* (pp. 31–40). New Directions for Continuing Education, no. 25. San Francisco: Jossey-Bass.

Brookfield, S. D. (1984). Self-directed adult learning: A critical paradigm. *Adult Education Quarterly, 35*(2), 59–71.

Brookfield, S. D. (Ed.). (1985). *Self-directed learning: From theory to practice.* New Directions for Continuing Education, no. 25. San Francisco: Jossey-Bass.

Brookfield, S. D. (1986). *Understanding and facilitating adult learning.* San Francisco: Jossey-Bass.

Brookfield, S. D. (1987). *Developing critical thinkers.* San Francisco: Jossey-Bass.

Brophy, J. (1983). Conceptualizing student motivation. *Educational Psychologist, 18*(3), 200–215.

Brophy, J. (1987). Synthesis of research strategies for motivating students to learn. *Educational Leadership, 45*(2), 40–48.

Brue, C. (1985). Breaking the ice. *Training and Development Journal, 39*(6), 26–28.

Bryson, L. (1936). *Adult Education.* New York: American Book.

Caffarella, R., & O'Donnell, J. (1987). Self-directed adult learning: A critical paradigm revisited. *Adult Education Quarterly, 37*(4), 199–211.

Cameron, C. (1988). Identifying learning needs: Six methods adult educators can use. *Lifelong Learning: An Omnibus of Practice and Research, 11*(4), 25–28.

Cassivi, D. (1989). The education of adults: Maintaining a legacy. *Lifelong Learning: An Omnibus of Practice and Research, 12*(5), 8–10.

Cervero, R. (1988). *Effective continuing education for professionals.* San Francisco: Jossey-Bass.

Claxton, C., & Murrell, P. (1987). *Learning styles: Implications for improving educational practice.* (ASHE-ERIC Higher Education Report 4). Washington, D.C.: ASHE-ERIC Clearinghouse on Higher Education.

Conti, G. (1985). Assessing teaching style in adult education: How and why. *Lifelong Learning: An Omnibus of Practice and Research, 8*(8), 7–11, 28.

Conti, G. (1990). Identifying your teaching style. In M. W. Galbraith (Ed.), *Adult learning methods: A guide for effective instruction* (pp. 79–96). Malabar, FL: Krieger.

Cornett, C. (1983). *What you should know about teaching and learning styles.* Bloomington: Phi Delta Kappa.

Cross, K. P. (1981). *Adults as learners.* San Francisco: Jossey-Bass.

Daloz, L. (1986). *Effective teaching and mentoring.* San Francisco: Jossey-Bass.

Deci, E., & Ryan, R. (1985). *Intrinsic motivation and self-determination in human behavior.* New York: Plenum.

Deshler, D. (Ed.). (1984). *Evaluation for program improvement.* New Directions for Continuing Education, no. 24. San Francisco: Jossey-Bass.

Dewey, J. (1916). *Democracy and education.* New York: Macmillan.

Dickinson, G. (1973). *Teaching adults: A handbook for instructors.* Don Mills: General Publishing.

Dixon, N. (1985). The implementation of learning style information. *Lifelong Learning: An Omnibus of Practice and Research, 9*(3), 16–18, 26.

Draves, W. (1984). *How to teach adults.* Manhattan, KS: Learning Resource Network.

Egan, G. (1975). *The skilled helper: A model for systematic helping and interpersonal relating.* Monterey: Brooks/Cole.

Egan, G. (1986). *The skilled helper: A systematic approach to effective helping* (3rd ed.). Monterey: Brooks/Cole.

Elias, J., & Merriam, S. (1980). *Philosophical foundations of adult education.* Malabar, FL: Krieger.

Ennis, C., Mueller, L., Hettrick, D., Chepyator-Thomson, J., Zhang, X., Rudd, W., Zhu, W., Ruhm, C., & Bebetsos, G. (1989). Educational climate in elective adult education: Shared decision making and communication patterns. *Adult Education Quarterly, 39*(2), 76–88.

Freire, P. (1970). *Pedagogy of the oppressed.* New York: Herder and Herder.

Galbraith, M. W. (1987). Assessing perceptual learning styles. In C. Klevins (Ed.), *Materials and methods in adult and continuing education* (pp. 263–269). Los Angeles: Klevens.

Galbraith, M. W. (1989). Essential skills for the facilitator of adult learning. *Lifelong Learning: An Omnibus of Practice and Research, 12*(6), 10–13.

Galbraith, M. W. (1990a). Attributes and skills of an adult educator. In M. W. Galbraith (Ed.), *Adult learning methods: A guide for effective instruction* (pp. 3–22). Malabar, FL: Krieger.

Galbraith, M. W. (Ed.). (1990b). *Adult learning methods: A guide for effective instruction.* Malabar, FL: Krieger.

Galbraith, M. W., & Sanders, R. E. (1987). Relationship between perceived learning style and teaching style of junior college educators. *Community/Junior College Quarterly of Research and Practice, 11*(3), 169–177.

Hayes, E. (Ed.). (1989). *Effective teaching styles.* New Directions for Continuing Education, no. 43. San Francisco: Jossey-Bass.

Hiemstra, R. (1988). Translating personal values and philosophy into practical action. In R. Brockett (Ed.), *Ethical issues in adult education* (pp. 178–194). New York: Teachers College Press.

Houle, C. (1972). *The design of education.* San Francisco: Jossey-Bass.

Hughes, J., Graham, S., & Galbraith, M. (1986). Adult development: A multifaceted approach. *The Journal of Continuing Higher Education, 34*(3), 24–28.

James, W., & Galbraith, M. W. (1985). Perceptual learning styles: Implications and techniques for the practitioner. *Lifelong Learning: An Omnibus of Practice and Research, 8*(4), 20–23.

Jarvis, P. (1987). *Adult learning in the social context.* London: Croom Helm.

Kanfer, F., & Goldstein, A. (Ed.). (1986). *Helping people change* (3rd ed.). New York: Pergamon.

Keller, J. (1987). Strategies for stimulating motivation to learn. *Performance and Instruction, 26*(8), 1–7.

Kidd, J. R. (1973). *How adults learn.* New York: Cambridge.

Klevins, C. (Ed.). (1987). *Materials and methods in adult and continuing education.* Los Angeles: Klevens.

Knowles, M. S. (1975). *Self-directed learning.* New York: Association Press.

Knowles, M. S. (1980). *The modern practice of adult education: From pedagogy to andragogy* (revised and updated). New York: Cambridge.

Knowles and Associates. (1984). *Andragogy in action: Applying modern principles of adult learning.* San Francisco: Jossey-Bass.

Knox, A. B. (1977). *Adult development and learning.* San Francisco: Jossey-Bass.

Knox, A. B. (Ed.). (1980). *Teaching adults effectively.* New Directions for Continuing Education, no. 6. San Francisco: Jossey-Bass.

Knox, A. B. (1986). *Helping adults learn: A guide to planning, implementing, and conducting programs.* San Francisco: Jossey-Bass.

Kolb, D. (1984). *Experiential learning: Experience as the source of learning and development.* Englewood Cliffs: Prentice-Hall.

Krupp, J. (1982). *The adult learner: A unique entity.* Manchester: Adult Development and Learning.

Lean, E. (1984). Color me training. *Training and Development Journal, 38*(3), 42–51.

Lewis, L. (Ed.). (1986). *Experiential and simulation techniques for teaching adults.* New Directions for Continuing Education, no. 30. San Francisco: Jossey-Bass.

Lincoln, Y., & Guba, E. (1985). *Naturalistic inquiry.* Beverly Hills: Sage.

Lindeman, E. C. (1926). *The meaning of adult education.* New York: New Republic.

Long, H. B. (1983). *Adult learning.* New York: Cambridge.

Long, H. B. (1990). Understanding adult learners. In M. W. Galbraith (Ed.), *Adult learning methods: A guide for effective instruction* (pp. 23–37). Malabar, FL: Krieger.

Long, H. B. and Associates (1988). *Self-directed learning: Application and theory.* Athens: Department of Adult Education, University of Georgia.

Marsick, V. (Ed.). (1987). *Learning in the workplace.* London: Croom Helm.

Marsick, V. (1988). Learning in the workplace: The case for reflectivity and critical reflectivity. *Adult Education Quarterly, 38*(4), 187–198.

McKenzie, L. (1985). Philosophical orientations of adult education. *Lifelong Learning: An Omnibus of Practice and Research, 9*(1), 18–20.

Merriam, S. (Ed.). (1982). *Linking philosophy and practice.* New Directions of Continuing Education, no. 15. San Francisco: Jossey-Bass.

Merriam, S. (Ed.). (1984a). *Selected writings on philosophy and adult education.* Malabar, FL: Krieger.

Merriam, S. (1984b). *Adult development: Implications for adult education*. Columbus: ERIC Clearinghouse on Adult, Career, and Vocational Education.

Merriam, S. (1987). Adult learning and theory building: A review. *Adult Education Quarterly, 37*(4), 187–198.

Mezirow, J. (1981). A critical theory of adult learning and education. *Adult Education, 32*(1), 3–23.

Mezirow, J. (1985). A critical theory of self-directed learning. In S. D. Brookfield (Ed.), *Self-directed learning: From theory to practice* (pp. 17–30). New Directions for Continuing Education, no. 25. San Francisco: Jossey-Bass.

Mezirow, J. and Associates. (1990). *Fostering critical reflection in adulthood*. San Francisco: Jossey-Bass.

Patterson, B. H. (1986). Creativity and andragogy: A boon for adult learners. *Journal of Creative Behavior, 20*(2), 99–109.

Peck, M. S. (1979). *The road less traveled*. New York: Simon and Schuster.

Podeschi, R. (1986). Philosophies, practices and American values. *Lifelong Learning: An Omnibus for Practice and Research, 9*(4), 4–6, 27–28.

Price, G. (1983). Diagnosing learning styles. In R. M. Smith (Ed.), *Helping adults learn how to learn* (pp. 49–55). San Francisco: Jossey-Bass.

Robinson, R. (1979). *An introduction to helping adults learn and change*. Milwaukee: Omnibook.

Rogers, C. (1969). *Freedom to learn*. Columbus: Merrill.

Rosenblum, S. (Ed.). (1985). *Involving adults in the educational process*. New Directions for Continuing Education, no. 26. San Francisco: Jossey-Bass.

Schlossberg, N., Lynch, A., & Chickering, A. (1989). *Improving higher education environments for adults*. San Francisco: Jossey-Bass.

Schön, D. (1983). *The reflective practitioner*. New York: Basic Books.

Schön, D. (1987). *Educating the reflective practitioner*. San Francisco: Jossey-Bass.

Scriven, M. (1972). Pros and cons about goal-free evaluation. *Evaluation Comment, 3*(4), 1–4.

Seaman, D., & Fellenz, R. (1989). *Effective strategies for teaching adults*. Columbus: Merrill.

Smith, R. (1982). *Learning how to learn.* New York: Cambridge.

Sork, T. (1987). Ethics and action. In C. Klevins (Ed.), *Materials and methods in adult and continuing education* (pp. 50–55). Los Angeles: Klevens.

Spear, G., & Mocker, D. (1984). The organizing circumstance: Environmental determinants in self-directed learning. *Adult Education Quarterly, 35*(1), 1–10.

Tagiuri, R. (1968). The concept of organizational climate. In R. Tagiuri & G. Litwin (Eds.), *Organizational climate: Exploration of a concept* (pp. 11–31). Boston: Harvard University, Division of Research, Graduate School of Business Administration.

Tough, A. (1979). *The adult's learning projects: A fresh approach to theory and practice in adult learning.* Toronto: Ontario Institute for Studies in Education.

Vosko, R. (1984). Shaping spaces for lifelong learning. *Lifelong Learning: An Omnibus of Practice and Research, 8*(2), 4–7, 28.

Wildemeersch, D., & Leirman, W. (1988). The facilitation of the life-world transformation. *Adult Education Quarterly, 39*(1), 19–30.

Wilson, J. (Ed.). (1983). *Materials for teaching adults: Selection, development, and use.* New Directions for Continuing Education, no. 17. San Francisco: Jossey-Bass.

Wlodkowski, R. (1985). *Enhancing adult motivation to learn.* San Francisco: Jossey-Bass.

Wlodkowski, R. (1990). Strategies to enhance adult motivation to learn. In M. W. Galbraith (Ed.), *Adult learning methods: A guide for effective instruction* (pp. 97–118). Malabar, FL: Krieger.

Zemke, R., & Kramlinger, T. (1982). *Figuring things out: A trainer's guide to needs and task analysis.* Reading: Addison-Wesley.

Zinn, L. (1983). Development of a valid and reliable instrument to identify a personal philosophy of adult education. *Dissertation Abstracts International, 44,* 1667A–1668A. University Microfilms No. DA 8323851.

Zinn, L. (1990). Identifying your philosophical orientation. In M. W. Galbraith (Ed.), *Adult learning methods: A guide for effective instruction* (pp. 39–77). Malabar, FL: Krieger.

CHAPTER 2

Grounding Teaching in Learning
STEPHEN BROOKFIELD

This chapter explores an idea breathtaking in its obviousness and simplicity. This idea, briefly stated, is that for teachers to be effective they should be aware of how learners experience learning. Most teacher training programs, however, are premised on an entirely different assumption—that for teachers to be effective they should be aware of theories and models of teaching. Hence, teacher training programs typically focus on studying exemplary teaching practices, on practicing a variety of pedagogic approaches, and on exploring models of instruction. When the experience of learning is considered it is usually in the context of broad theories of psychological functioning or personality development—behaviorism, humanistic psychotherapy, stage theory, life-span development, and so on. The actual experience of learning as felt and reported by learners themselves is rendered relatively unimportant. In this chapter I will outline an approach to teaching that places the experience of learning as reported by learners themselves at its center. This approach to teaching I call grounded teaching.

THE CONCEPT OF GROUNDED TEACHING

The concept of grounded teaching is derived from that of grounded theory, a qualitative approach to collecting and analyzing research data. In a grounded theory approach, data collection and data analysis are concurrent. Researchers develop tentative hypotheses, organizing concepts, and theories about the topic they are investigating at the same time as they are collecting data. They pause

33

regularly in the research process to take stock and to decide what to do next. Which themes to pursue, what data to collect, which emerging hypotheses to test, and when to change direction are decisions which are constantly made, and changed, as part of a continuous research process. There is no predetermined end point to the research activity. It is open-ended, and grounded theorists decide when the organizing theoretical categories they are investigating have become "saturated" with sufficient data.

Grounded teaching is the pedagogic equivalent of grounded theory. It is not governed by the doggedly relentless pursuit of a previously specified learning objective, though it certainly is informed by a sense of purpose and direction. But while grounded teachers have an organizing vision of where the educational effort should be going, they are flexible and adaptive, responding to learners' needs, interests, and perceptions as these emerge. Teachers and learners stop regularly to take stock of which content themes, and which methods, to try next. Grounded teachers ask learners how their actions as teachers are perceived, what classroom events are remembered by learners as learning "peaks," and what events are remembered as alienating or infantilizing to learners. Hence, the organizing concern of grounded teachers is to elicit from learners how learning feels. As with the grounded theory approach to research, there is a praxis of action and analysis. What to explore next and how to explore it are decisions that are made in the midst of the activity so that curricula and methods are continually scrutinized and renegotiated in the light of learners' perceptions of their learning processes.

This kind of teaching is inductive and inferential. It is a qualitatively inclined pedagogy in sharp contrast to teaching premised on the linear pursuit of previously specified, clear-cut learning objectives. Consequently, it is harder to explain to neophytes, and harder to justify to administrators, than teaching derived from positivist, quantifiable approaches to learning. Grounded teachers find it difficult to submit detailed descriptions of the precise activities that will occur in classroom sessions extending over weeks and months, since what actually happens is certain to differ to a greater or lesser degree from what was planned. This means that grounded teachers must be tolerant of ambiguity, since they cannot specify the precise outcomes of every meeting before it happens. This often raises political difficulties for teachers inclined to use this approach, since institutions, curricula, and educational programs (particularly those where licensing or credentialing are involved) are based on models of teaching and learning which demand the specification of clear behavioral objectives before the educational activity begins.

The most important characteristic of grounded teaching is that it is based on an understanding of, concern for, and attention to the learner's experience of learning. Grounded teachers assume that it is crucially important to understand, for example, how it feels to learners to explore unfamiliar intellectual territory; what symbolic importance learners attribute to various teacher actions; what peaks and lows they discern in a learning episode; how they live through the excitements, boredom, fears, and frustrations of learning something difficult; and what they remember as being of most significance to them (rather than to teachers) about educational events. Grounded teachers make a systematic attempt to elicit from learners their perceptions of the learning process through such means as interviews, learning journals, and critical incidents. Hence, grounded teaching is a phenomenological pedagogy, which emphasizes the need to understand learners' perceptions of their own learning in the terms in which they frame these. Teachers' actions are informed by an appreciation of how learning processes are experienced by learners. In grounded teaching primacy is given to learners' perceptions of what is significant about learning and the educational process as much as it is to predetermined objectives and preselected methods.

SOURCES FOR GROUNDED TEACHING

Three sources have clearly contributed to the central themes of grounded teaching explored later in this chapter. These sources are (1) descriptive analyses of learning completed by participants in workshops on adult learning; (2) learning journals compiled by adult learners; and (3) documented accounts of the experience of learning as described by learners. Let me say something, very briefly, about each of these.

Descriptive Analyses of Learning

In workshops on adult learning which I have run over the years at Teachers College, Columbia University, New York, I have asked participants who have taken these for credit to write an assignment analyzing their own learning. Although most of these participants are practicing teachers, I have asked them to draw on their experiences as learners within formal educational classes and to write about learning episodes within those which they remembered as being somehow significant. Those who have been willing to do so have allowed me to keep copies of their assignments for research purposes, and I have drawn on these for this chapter. The assignment asks participants to answer the questions below which focus mostly on critical incidents in their own educational life histories.

Example. Think back over the last experience you had as a learner in an educational program. Describe, in as specific, concrete and descriptive a fashion as possible:

1. The incident, or incidents, that you recall as being most exciting and rewarding in that they represented learning "highs" for you—times when you felt that something important and significant was happening to you as a learner.

2. The incident, or incidents, that you recall as being the most distressing or disappointing in that they represented learning "lows" for you.

3. The characteristics and behaviors of teachers that you found most helpful to your learning. Give specific examples of events when these characteristics and behaviors were observable.

4. The characteristics and behaviors of teachers that you found hindered your learning. Give specific examples of events when these characteristics and behaviors were observable.

5. Those times when, as a learner, you felt valued and affirmed.

6. Those times when, as a learner, you felt demeaned and infantilized.

7. The most important insights you realized about yourself as a learner.

8. The most important insights you realized about the nature of effective teaching.

9. The most pleasurable aspects of learning you experienced.

10. The most distressing aspects of learning you experienced.

11. The resources you found most useful—human and material.

Now, analyze the information you've given in response to these questions with regard to the following themes:

a. The common themes that seem to emerge from your descriptions about the kinds of learning experiences that are most useful to you.

b. The common themes that seem to emerge from your descriptions about the kinds of learning experiences that are least useful to you.

c. The advice you would give to a new learner on how to survive and succeed within education.

d. The advice you would give to a teacher on methods and personal characteristics which would be most helpful to learners.

Learning Journals

Learning journals are a valuable source of information about how learners experience learning, yet because of the time it takes learners to reflect on their experiences and record these in writing, this technique is rather neglected. Unless the keeping of such journals is mandated (which runs the risk of turning the activity into required busywork, thereby rendering it useless) adult students often have little time to spend recording their perceptions of their own learning processes. Yet the effort to do this is very worthwhile, not only for the learner as an exercise in reflective analysis, but for teachers who are seeking to gain some sense of the emotional tenor of their groups. Learning journals provide an immediate and direct recounting of learners' experiences of learning, relatively undistorted by teacher or researcher interventions. For example, Fingeret's (1983) description of her culture shock as a practitioner entering graduate school, and the attitudinal shifts she experienced regarding her own abilities, her self-concept as a learner, and the validity of academic study to "real life" during this episode in her life, is a vividly graphic depiction of the psychological odyssey of one person's transformational learning. It reads with a potency and validity which is much more striking than survey reports of the same phenomenon en masse. When I have asked students in the graduate program at Teachers College to analyze Fingeret's description of her experiences, they frequently respond by talking about the points of congruence between their own reactions to graduate school and hers, and of how they recognized aspects of themselves in her account. Hence, although her account is one person's description of what was perceived as a highly idiosyncratic experience, it has embedded within it many generic elements which are recognized by successive intakes of graduate students.

Despite the connective power of learning journals and the vivid way they can help teachers appreciate how learners experience learning, few efforts have been made to use them in adult education. However, provided that instructions for keeping journals are kept clear and simple, and avoid phenomenological jargon, learners should not find it too onerous or time-consuming to maintain a brief but highly revealing journal. In my own practice I ask learners to jot down a few comments after each class session:

1. What they experienced as the chief learning "high" of the session—what activity, insight, or teacher action enthused, enlightened, or excited them the most.

2. What they experienced as the chief learning "low" of the session—what activity, insight, or teacher action distressed, bored, or angered them the most.

3. What, if anything, they feel they gained from the session.

4. What, if anything, they felt a sense of a missed opportunity over.

5. Anything they noticed about changes or developments in their own learning activities, processes, or responses.

These journals are anonymous and are read only by me. Their contents are kept in confidence and are not shared with other students unless the writers agree, and even then the identities of the writers are disguised. Additionally, students are encouraged to record their reflections on their long-term development as learners, unconnected to particular class sessions, and this kind of analysis is arguably the most valuable of all. But realistically, teachers cannot rely on these kinds of longitudinally reflective journals being compiled, whereas the responses to the five questions outlined above take very little time to complete immediately after a session. Teachers cannot assume, of course, that learners' perceptions revealed in learning journals are wholly inclusive and authentic in terms of integrating all possible perspectives on a situation. It would be foolish to think that all learners are either immediately comfortable with keeping such journals or sophisticated in doing this. But if learners get into the habit of writing brief journal entries to these five questions, and allowing teachers to read these privately, they can help teachers enormously in the very difficult effort of trying to appreciate how learners experience learning in the most accurate way possible.

Accounts of the Experience of Learning

In recent years there has been a growing interest in recording learners' direct perceptions of their learning experiences. As a concept, experiential learning has become an accepted part of the educational lexicon, and it has occurred to many researchers that it is just as important to study learning from the learner's viewpoint as it is to study how teachers view their students' learning. Three important anthologies on *Reflective Learning* (Boud, Keogh, & Walker, 1984), *Appreciating Adults Learning* (Boud & Griffin, 1987) and *Developing Student Autonomy in Learning* (Boud, 1988) contain descriptions of learning episodes from the perspective of learners "inside" those episodes. A number of dissertations at the Ontario Institute for Studies in Education have explored this same theme in a variety of educational contexts (Bates, 1970; Denis, 1979; Taylor, 1979; Boyd, 1981; Griffith, 1982; Gehrels, 1984; Robinson, Saberton, & Griffin, 1985; D'Andrea, 1985; Barer-Stein, 1985). Then there are a number of other studies focusing on how women experience learning (Mezirow, 1978; Belenky, Clinchy, Goldberger, & Tarule, 1986; Persico, 1988; Hutchinson & Hutchinson, 1988; Rannells Saul, 1989), on adult students "best" and "worst" classroom learning experiences (Sheckley, 1988), on how Native American learners perceive teachers' actions (Conti & Fellenz, 1988), on cross-cultural analyses of learners' perceptions of learning (Pratt, 1988, 1989), on the experiences of students in a "second chance" program for working class adults (Edwards, 1986), on how literacy students view success and failure (Charnley & Jones, 1981; Van Tilburg & DuBois, 1989), on adult students' perceptions of teachers' attempts to negotiate curricula with them (Millar, Morphett, & Saddington, 1987) and on how the activities of self-taught adult learners contradict much of the espoused theory in this area (Brookfield, 1981; Danis & Tremblay, 1988; Spear, 1988). Insights drawn from all these studies have contributed to the grounded teaching approach outlined in this chapter.

HOW LEARNERS EXPERIENCE LEARNING

The insights into the experience of learning described in this section are highly tentative and provisional. Needless to say, they are also ethnocentric, representing only the reported experience of learning of a small number of English speaking adult students in formal educational programs in the United States, Canada, Britain, Australia, and New Zealand. They are in no sense statistically representative of the larger population of adults in these societies, let alone the world. On such flimsy empirical foundations it would be foolish indeed to claim for these insights anything remotely approaching a "theory" of adult learning. But these insights are important to the extent that they provide a stronger empirical footing for even very limited, contextually specific generalizations regarding teaching adults, than do the sweeping prescriptions for good practice found in many texts on teaching. With the caveats mentioned above, let me take what seem to be the most interesting elements of how adults experience learning which seem to have the greatest replicability across the three sources and multitude of contexts in which these experiences are reported.

The Impostor Syndrome

From adult basic education students to students in doctoral adult education programs, there is a very commonly reported perception of adult learners within formal education that they should not really be there, that they are somehow "impostors." Learners report how at the beginning of a new course or program they wrestle with whether or not to continue when they see how capable all the other students are. They feel that there has been some kind of mistake made in their being there at all. Ironically a great number of new adult students feel this sense of having entered a program under false pretences, yet perceive everyone else as being much more capable and confident than themselves. This feeling of being undeserving impostors who will sooner or later have their real, pathetically inadequate identities revealed is remarkably consistent across the contexts discussed in the three sources above. In my own practice I had expected such levels of anxiety and insecurity among adult basic education students or those stereotypically labelled as "disadvantaged." It has been a revelation to encounter such feelings among intake after intake of doctoral students, all of whom are senior professionals occupying positions of great power and responsibility in their lives outside of the doctoral study environment.

Speculatively, it seems as if there is a strong element of authority-dependence in many adults' socialization which predisposes them to regress to childlike behavior upon entering an adult classroom. Adults returning to formal education should not be seen as lions of self-directedness, roaring to escape the leash of teacher and institutionally imposed constraints. Many of them seem to perceive themselves as inadequate impostors who wish to hide their inadequacies as best they can by seizing on cues tossed off by teachers about what behaviors are expected of students. What strikes me about this impostor syndrome is how much it parallels my own experience, not only as a learner, but as a supposed "expert" on adult learning and education. Whenever I am asked to address a group of practitioners, or give a keynote speech at a conference, I ask myself what I can possibly offer that can have any relevance or use to people. The people I meet at such gatherings seem to have such a wealth of experience, and to be working in such insightful and innovative ways, that I doubt whether anything I can say will have any meaning or validity for them. I feel, in effect, like an impostor who, as soon as he starts speaking, will send the people who arranged for his visit into paroxyms of embarrassment at their lapse of judgment. Admittedly this can be interpreted as grandiose self-importance masked as an appealing modesty. But I believe that many more teachers experience this impostor syndrome at various times than those who do not.

Connectedness

Learning is frequently spoken of in highly emotional terms by adults describing their experiences. This hardly seems surprising, yet the emotional dimensions to learning receive scant attention indeed in formal research on adult education. Adults' reflections on how learning feels run the emotional gamut, from profound embarrassment at their inabilities to seem as assured and confident as they feel they ought, to deep, angry resentment at the dismissive arro-

gance displayed by teachers, or exhilarating relief and pleasure at
being able to perform some task previously thought impenetrable.
From inside a learning event, learners speak of their stumbling
across an insight, or making some important connection, in very
physiological terms. They speak about getting chills, about hair
standing up on the back of their necks, or about their pulses racing
with excitement. Equally, they talk about feeling flushed with anger,
hot with embarrassment, or of a painful knot of anxiety forming
inside their stomachs as they perceive themselves to be falling short
of self-imposed or teacher prescribed standards. Learning is rarely
experienced in an anodyne, emotionally denuded way. This is in
contrast to education which often is spoken of as nothing so much
as exhaustingly, mind-numblingly boring. It is evident that to many
adults the activity of teachers teaching sometimes has little to do
with that of learners learning.

When learners speak about learning episodes which they remember with some emotion and which they recall vividly, the element of connectedness is frequently evident. By connectedness I
mean that the event or episode has some deeply felt meaning for
them. Sometimes learners use the concept of relevance to describe
this sense of connection, but they do not always mean relevance in
some strictly vocational sense of job utility. They mean instead that
an idea, practice, or task is interpreted as revelatory to them in that
it helps them to understand something about themselves or about
their situations which perhaps they had not fully perceived before.
Or that they come to interpret events or situations in what are seen
as wholly new, and more accurate, ways. Or that the educational
activity undertaken parallels something in their own lives. Episodes
of activity or reflection in which this sense of connectedness is felt
are remembered as learning peaks.

This concept of connectedness is hardly new in adult education. It is the focus of the oft-quoted injunction to "start where the
students are" and its importance is attested to by adult educators as
ideologically diverse as Paulo Freire, Malcolm Knowles, and Cyril
Houle. The concept of connectedness has also received attention in
Belenky et al.'s *Women's Ways of Knowing* (1986), which elaborates
the concept of connected teaching as an alternative mode of teaching
which women will find more congenial. Connected teaching is not
the same as giving students what they say they want. As Belenky et al.
comment "a connected teacher is not just another student; the role

carries special responsibilities" (p. 227). Teachers are connected if they "emphasize connection over separation, understanding and acceptance over assessment, and collaboration over debate: if they accord respect to and allow time for the knowledge that emerges from firsthand experience; if instead of imposing their own expectations and arbitrary requirements, they encourage students to evolve their own patterns of work based on the problems they are pursuing" (p. 229). The importance of connectedness attested to by the women in the *Women's Ways of Knowing* sample is present in the responses of both men and women in the three sources for grounded teaching used for this chapter. It is not gender-specific.

Episodes of Challenge

When asked to speak about significant learning episodes—those which are remembered vividly as being crucial and which are spoken about with pride—it is interesting that many adults speak of episodes in which challenge was a central feature. They will choose events and occasions when they were faced with difficult situations or with dilemmas which had no clearly resolvable solutions. These might be situations in which they were required to explore areas of knowledge which they found intimidating. Or times when they had to learn new skills which did not come easily to them. Or occasions when they were forced to explore a world view or interpretative frame of reference, with which they did not feel comfortable. These challenging episodes were ones in which learners felt themselves somehow exposed and ones in which a high degree of risk was involved. They are regarded as transformative turning points, which lead to changes in the individual's self-concept as a learner. What is recalled with such satisfaction is the way in which the challenges were faced and dealt with so that the learners felt they had successfully survived a problematic situation. Such an experience is truly empowering. Areas which were previously viewed as being "out of bounds" to learners are reinterpreted as being within their purview. They come to see themselves as being potentially able to act upon such areas, rather than being closed off from them.

The emotional tenor of these episodes is complex. As adults recall them they speak of the threats to the ego entailed by exploring problematic areas of knowledge, new skill sets, or unfamiliar interpretative frameworks. Yet it is the newly revealed capacity to survive these endeavours successfully that is remembered with such pride.

An important aspect of these episodes is the exhilaratingly liberating feeling of being able to survive experiences (such as passing a statistics exam, writing a philosophy paper, getting through the first week of a teaching career, confronting authority figures such as professors, giving a spoken presentation in front of a group of peers, or defending a thesis to a hostile committee) which had previously been perceived as terrifying and totally beyond a learner's capability. Following on from this is a sense of increased self-confidence. A sense that "well, if I can do this then maybe this other area I've always been frightened of isn't going to be so difficult after all." What to a teacher might appear an accomplishment of very little significance—such as writing a letter using a word processor, an adult nonreader writing the name of a favorite baseball team, or a nonswimmer spluttering down the swimming pool to touch the tiling at the end of a lap for the first time—might be experienced by the people involved as breakthrough events in terms of their self-images as learners.

Reflective Speculation

One of the most frequently espoused principles of effective practice in teaching adults is that of praxis—that is, of ensuring that opportunities for action and reflection are available in a balanced way for learners. Praxis means that curricula are not studied in some kind of artificial isolation, but that ideas, skills, and insights learned in a classroom are tested and experienced actively in real contexts. Essential to praxis is the opportunity for reflection on experience, so that formal study is informed by some appreciation of the imperatives of real life contexts. Although the apparent division of action and reflection in praxis is conceptually clean, it is not paralleled in reality. Schön's (1983) concept of reflection-in-action is especially important in this regard since it elaborates on how practitioners reflect on events while "inside" them.

What is interesting to note with regard to accounts of how learners experience learning in formal educational settings is the lack of time and opportunity for reflective speculation these learners report in their courses, workshops, and institutes. Despite the frequency with which the principle of praxis is espoused within the literature of adult education, in reality it seems that the action component of praxis is given far more emphasis than that of reflection. Learners typically say that teachers rush through masses of content and that assignments designed to assess learners' familiarity with this content come so thick and fast that there is barely time to assimilate new ideas and knowledge, let alone reflect on them. There is apparently little chance for learners to interpret what they are being exposed to in terms of their past experiences or to trace connections between new ideas and perspectives and their developed meaning schemes. The "mulling over" period reported as being so important for learners to make interpretive sense of what is happening to them is neglected. In terms of models of experiential learning (Kolb, 1984) it is as if the cycle of concrete experience, reflection on that experience, abstract conceptualization, and application of insights in new contexts is broken by learners not experiencing fully the reflective observation or abstract conceptualization components. One of the most frequently reported lamentations of learners after they have completed a formal educational course is how the richness of the experience was reduced so drastically by their being forced to do too much in too short a time. Teachers seem to err in favor of breadth over depth, no doubt because of frequently being constrained by the requirements of accrediting bodies, licensing arrangements, the need to fit learners into a series of institutionally prescribed, progressively taken curricula, and so on. A consequence of this is that learners report feeling that they have never really "comes to grips" with a new knowledge or skill area. They have never learned the "grammar" of the activity they are immersed in; that is, they never learned the basic internal criteria, organizing concepts, and broad categorizations endemic to the bodies of knowledge or skill sets they are studying.

These comments do not come across as lazy students carping about the perfectly fair requirements of conscientious teachers. Rather, they are expressed with a sense of regret that what could have been such a meaningful and connected experience was rendered so fleeting and unsatisfactory by the lack of opportunity for reflective speculation on what was being learned. Learners intuitively sense that reflection and action need to be balanced for them to make the most of an educational event, and when the reflective component is neglected so drastically they experience a marked diminution of the richness of the event. Learners also report an overemphasis on the action component of praxis in their experience of classroom activities. They speak of endless small group exercises which seem to be used for no discernible reason other than that the educator feels that this is somehow expected. Far from being an

experience which increases the intensity, connectedness, and richness of the educational event, small group work is often perceived
as meaningless busy work, and not infrequently interpreted as a
sign of teachers' laziness, unpreparedness, lack of expertise, or insecurity. The inference is often made by adult learners that the use of
small group methods betokens nothing so much as a teacher's re-
fusal to do the preparation necessary to "proper" teaching.

One of the greatest, and most ironic, theory-practice discrep-
ancies in teaching adults is the way in which teachers of adults rush
to use small group exercises in the belief that adults will appreciate
these because (a) their experience as people is being dignified and
(b), they will feel much easier about participating in small group
discussion than discussion in larger groups. In reality, the un-
doubted value of small group work is lost if teachers rush to this too
early in the belief that if they don't use this method then adult
learners will feel insulted by the evident authoritarianism of the
teacher. In fact in learning journals and critical incident accounts of
educational participation, adult learners frequently speak of feeling
insulted by an overuse of small group work. Their sense of insult
comes from the perception that teachers have "dumped" the responsibility for learning on learners, when the predominant feeling these
learners are experiencing is one of being awash in ambiguity and
confusion. They speak and write of their sense of relief at sometimes
being able to occupy the role of attentive listener as an expert who
has spend some considerable time exploring an area of intellectual
concern lays out its conceptual topography for them. They appreciate the opportunity for reflective speculation afforded by the lecture
approach and use metaphors such as "luxuriating" in the chance to
listen to someone talking in an interesting and informed way about
ideas which interest both teacher and learner.

The use of the term *luxuriate* in these accounts is particularly
interesting because it encapsulates an erroneous assumption about
the nature of learning to which teachers and learners both subscribe. Briefly stated, this assumption is that unless learners are seen
to be learning then an educational event is of little validity. Put
another way, unless learners are exhibiting the behaviors associated
with actively engaged, participatory learning (such as talking animat-
edly in small groups) then they are experiencing something less than
the appropriate level of fulfillment they should derive from the
educational activity. Based on this assumption it is easy to see why

teachers and learners should view episodes of reflective speculation as a luxury. It is almost as if learner silence is equated with mental inertia. Hence, teachers rush to fill the supposed vacuum of learner inertia with small group activities. And they equate the degree of animation exhibited by small group participants with intellectual alertness. How often have you come across a classroom in which there is total silence? And if you did, would not your first inference be that there was something seriously wrong there? Yet, if we take the idea of praxis seriously, or if we give any credence to models of experiential learning, then periods of reflective analysis and speculation must be granted equal importance with periods of active engagement. Learners themselves would certainly seem to prefer many more opportunities for such reflective speculation and analysis, either through teachers slowing down in their eagerness to cover prescribed content, or through their willingness to allow reflective interludes in their classes. Taken to its logical extreme, this would mean that a small group discussion which was most productively connected for learners would be one distinguished by periods of silence as well as heated conversation. A revolutionary idea indeed to adherents of participatory learning and democratic discussion! As one such adherent I have tried to act on these insights offered by learners about the need for reflective interludes and allow many more periods of silence in classes. These can be disguised as coffee or stretch breaks if learners are as uncomfortable about the presence of silence in a classroom as teachers frequently are. Or one could switch on a tape recorder and play some unobtrusive music for these periods. But however it is done, it is worthwhile for teachers of adults to take the time to think about how to include greater opportunities for learners to undertake reflective analysis.

Transitional Fluctuation

Teachers often make curricula and instructional decisions premised on ideas about learning processes which do not parallel how learners experience learning. One example of this is the way so much attention is paid to arranging for curricula materials and instructional approaches which take learners through activities sequenced according to their progressively increased levels of complexity. The assumption seems to be that learning is experienced as a developmental process paralleling the progressive sequencing evident in curricula and instructional organization. In fact, learners often speak of significant learning episodes in terms which suggest a transitional fluctuation. This is particularly the case with critical thinking (Brookfield, 1987), but I venture that this experience is much more frequent in other domains that we typically acknowledge. In critical thinking adults make explicit some assumptions on which their habitual ways of thinking and acting have been based, and then begin to discard some of these assumptions and reframe others because they do not fit with their experience of reality. This process is seldom experienced sequentially in some neat developmental fashion. Instead, it is a case of "two steps forward, one step back." Learning critical thinking is a kind of transitional mambo. With a contradictory sense of liberation and fear, people venture into the process of trusting their inner voices of disquiet and confusion to the point where they discard erroneous assumptions and reframe existing ones to fit reality.

A frequently reported pattern is for someone to shift into another way of interpretating a habitual way of thinking or acting and to embrace this with the enthusiasm of release and liberation. This initial embracing is followed by the onset of fearful anxiety about the security of this new way of thinking or acting and a longing for the security of old assumptions. Feeling this way learners retreat to their familiar, and recently discarded, assumptive cluster with a sense of having "come home." But upon arriving home there is a sense things aren't the same anymore and that what previously gave comfort is now curiously unsatisfying. Sooner or later they are encouraged to venture again on the process of exploring new assumptions and reframing existing ones, but then at a certain point they experience again the terror of having the rug of familiar assumptions torn out from under them and they retreat back to more familiar assumptions, which are experienced again as not "fitting" anymore, and so on in a continuous fluctuating process. Finger (1988) has observed this process in how people decide to become adult educators, and he uses the metaphor of home and abroad to describe the way exploring an unfamilar assumptive territory is experienced. It is a telling metaphor and describes in colloquial terms the transitional fluctuations learners experience in venturing into new skill sets, areas of knowledge, and frameworks of interpretation. One of the most frequent reactions of someone travelling abroad for the first time is for them to feel an enhanced sense of their own uniqueness. Their very presence in an unfamiliar context heightens their perception of what were previously regarded as mundane everyday realities. They experience a longing for the familiar concurrent with their excitement at the unfamiliar. Much the same dialectical tension between the lure of the unknown and the appeal of the already known is felt by adults learning critical thinking.

One important aspect of this transitional fluctuation for teaching is that teachers who are aware of this typical rhythm are not discomforted when they see learners retreating to older and more habitual ways of thinking and behaving. To teachers unaware of this typical rhythm, the period of retreat might be mistakenly interpreted as an instance of regression or slippage, and regarded as evidence of teacher failure. There would be a mistaken but completely understandable attempt to rush in too quickly and force learners "back on track" by emphasizing the benefits of their newly learned assumptions. Knowing that such temporary retreats from actions and interpretations that were initially embraced with enthusiasm and passion are natural and inevitable in how learners experience the entry into the unfamiliar, relieves teachers of a great many unnecessary guilt feelings. They can use the returns to "home" as teachable moments for reflective analysis, so that learners gain greater insight into their learning patterns. Helping adults to develop insight into their habitual learning rhythms—what is known as learning how to learn or the development of epistemic cognition—is one of the most valuable and lasting effects teachers can have on people.

A Learning Community

It is remarkable how many adults use a survival metaphor when speaking of their experiences in formal adult and higher education. Education is frequently perceived as an intellectual orienteering exercise, in which students are dropped in the middle of unfamiliar curricular territory and expected to negotiate unknown and hostile terrain before finding the security of base camp. Adults recall their entrances into higher education with vivid memories of confusion, fear, and an inability to distinguish between friends or enemies in the anonymous and potentially hostile crowd clustered around them. They speak of their first experiences of education with the same sense of stunned alarm articulated by tourists who find themselves in the middle of the New York City subway system for the first time, only to discover that map guiding them through the system is back in the hotel room. They might look back on the experience with a feeling of pride that they made it through without serious, irreparable psychological or physical damage, but while they are living it their only thought is of surviving. When speaking of surviving adult and higher education the factor which is recalled more than any other as being important is the existence of a learning community. Sometimes this community takes the form of a dyadic partnership, sometimes it is a larger group of between four and eight in size. Whatever its size, however, this community functions as a support network of learners who reassure each other that the feelings of inadequacy, confusion, and depression they each experience are not idiosyncratic but shared by all. People will say how important it was to them to know that if they woke up at 3.00 a.m. suffering panic attacks about their inability to complete a course, perform a skill, give a presentation, write an essay, pass a statistics exam, or defend a thesis (to mention some of the more familiar events which held particular terror), that there was a person or group of people any one of whom would not mind being awakened by an anxiety stricken colleague in the small hours. In fact the emotional sustenance provided by this kind of peer support network was spoken of as being much more important than any information exchange function the community might have.

Knowing the importance of such emotionally sustaining support networks to adult learners is important. Teachers can seize on opportunities to assist the development of such networks whenever possible. They can encourage forms of peer teaching (Whitman, 1988). They can publish learners' names and addresses early on in an activity, so each one knows who lives in his or her home area. They can ask learners to write on poster paper what they feel are their most important skills and knowledge areas, what they would most like to learn, what enthusiasms inspire them, what dreams they have for the future and so on, and then display these publicly so that each learner gets some sense of the enthusiasms and interests of others in the group. Informal clustering will usually happen in the passage of time and one should be wary of forcing it at an unnaturally fast pace, but most teachers could probably pay considerably more attention to it than they habitually do. Teachers can also think about reorganizing some learning activities so that these might be accomplished as group activities. For example, in the doctoral program at Teachers College, Columbia University in which I currently work—the AEGIS program (Adult Education Through

Guided Independent Study)—we encourage doctoral students to formulate dissertations proposals, draft and field test instruments, conduct literature reviews, and sometimes even analyse each other's data in a collaborative dissertation group. Teachers might also consider the extent to which they can abolish or reduce formal grading of learners in their practice. In the AEGIS program we have abolished letter grades completely, moving to a pass fail system. One reason for doing this is our belief that if you want adults to cooperate in an educational project based on mutual inquiry then you must remove inducements to competitiveness from the situation. In classes where learners know that on a bell curve of grades only a limited number of "A" grades are available, people will be reluctant to share insights and information with each other, or "let their guard down" to reveal their sense of inadequacy, for fear of losing valuable ground in the quest for one of those prized high grades. A common reaction will be to ask "why should I let someone else get the benefit from all the effort I have put into this?" So competitive grading is directly antithetical to the creation of a supportive, emotionally sustaining learning community.

Teacher Credibility

This chapter is concerned with grounding teaching in learning, so emphasis has, of necessity, been placed on exploring how learners experience learning processes. It is important to note, however, that in speaking of significant, transformative learning events, learners often make explicit mention of how teachers' actions are crucial to their own learning. Central to their recollections is a characteristic which I describe as teacher credibility. Teacher credibility refers to the need for teachers to be perceived as having content mastery, expert knowledge, and depth of insight in the area in which they teach—of having "something to offer" learners. Learners repeatedly stress the wish to be in the presence of someone who is perceived as having greater factual knowledge, skill mastery, and reasoning facility than they (the learners) currently possess. They want to be with teachers whose breadth and depth of experience means that they can offer informed insights into the contradictions, complexities, and dilemmas learners are encountering.

This wish clearly contradicts much espoused adult education theory, which holds that the teacher's process skills are by far the most important for learners' development. To learners, however,

process skill without intellectual and experiential credibility is ultimately empty. In this regard it is interesting to reflect that the tendency of many teachers of adults to dignify the validity of learners'
experiences by belittling the significance of their own, can be a
serious mistake. Teachers may believe that in saying to learners
"look, my own experience possesses no greater innate validity than
yours" that they are encouraging in learners a valuing of their own
experiences. In actuality, exactly the reverse can happen. Protestations from teachers that they don't really know any more than
learners do, and that teachers are simply there to help learners
realize that they already possess the knowledge and skills they need,
sound supportive and respectful. But such protestations from teachers who are demonstrably more skillful, intellectually able, and
possessed of a much greater range of experience than that of learners will be perceived by those learners as false. Instead of learners
warming to what teachers believe to be admirably humane, respectful behavior to learners, these learners may conclude that if teachers' experiences have left them with no greater insight than that
possessed by learners, then there is nothing to be learned from
them. Hence, it is important that in our desire to affirm the validity
of learners' own experiences and abilities, we do not undercut our
own credibility in their eyes.

CONCLUSION

Grounding teaching in learning is neither easy nor convenient. Trying to do this countervails many prevailing organizational
assumptions. It means that objectives and methods cannot be
planned and outcomes predicted exactly months in advance of the
educational activity; that learning cannot be relied upon to take
place during certain hours each week; that evaluative criteria cannot be fixed at the outset of an educational activity and expected to
be as relevant at the end as at the beginning. Adopting a grounded
teaching approach means that teaching effectiveness becomes essentially a contextual judgment strongly informed by how learners
interpret what happens to them. And contextual notions of teaching effectiveness do not sit easily with the administrative desire to
standardize effectiveness in a series of easily replicable indicators.
So I realize that the process of trying to understand how learners

experience learning, analyzing how one can alter practice to take account of this understanding, and reframing purposes, methods, and evaluative criteria as dominant themes and concerns emerge from a group is complex, ambiguous, and institutionally inconvenient. Ideally teaching should be governed by what assists learning, not what is administratively neat, but in reality few of us have the opportunity to practice grounded teaching to the full extent outlined here.

Many teachers can find ways, however, of exploring how learners experience learning and of working creatively within their own contexts to make their practice more sensitive to this process. Using critical incidents and learning journals teachers can gain insights into this process relatively quickly and easily. The benefits to be gained from using these techniques to explore learners' learning processes seem to me to be enormous. At the very least, they alert teachers to common rhythms of learning and to the crucial turning points which are endemic to transformative change in learners. This means that we are less likely to make some of the more frequent mistakes committed in the name of good adult education practice, such as trying to halt learners' temporary retreats to "home" when experiencing unfamiliar activities, soft-pedalling our efforts to challenge learners because we feel they cannot survive these, or immediately rushing in to fill what we see as embarrassing vacuums of silence (and what to learners are important episodes of reflective speculation) with meaningless busy work which does little other than prove to ourselves that we are behaving like good adult educators are supposed to. It also means that we cannot avoid becoming aware of the tremendous complexity of teaching and learning, in particular of how what learners take from education, and what for them are crucially transformative learning events, are varied, idiosyncratic, and often unanticipated both by learners and teachers. Such a realization may in the short term be humbling and confusing, but in the long term it means that we develop a healthy habit of reflecting critically on the pronouncements of "experts." We realize the essential artificiality of standardized curricula, packaged materials, and evaluative indices prescribed from on high. We become much more attuned to acknowledging how context distorts the neat practice injunctions contained in textbooks such as this. And we cease to pursue the unproductive chimera of trying to discover the one method of adult education appropriate to all contexts, tasks,

and learners. In short, we stand more chance of attaining the congenial point of balance sought by all really good teachers—the balance of being both challenging and supportive, of having credibility
in learners' eyes because of what we have to offer, yet not being
afraid of admitting to error. We can find the balance of becoming
critically responsive teachers, on the one hand guided by values and
visions which we believe are important, but on the other hand
always open to reframing and renegotiating these as learners' own
values and visions emerge.

REFERENCES

Barer-Stein, T. (1985). *Learning as a process of experiencing difference*. Unpublished doctoral dissertation, Ontario Institute for
Studies in Education.

Bates, H. M. (1979). *A phenomenological study of adult learners:
Participants' experiences of a learner-centered approach*. Un-
published doctoral dissertation, Ontario Institute for Studies in
Education.

Belenky, M. F., Clinchy, B. M., Goldberger, N. R., & Tarule, J. M.
(1986). *Women's ways of knowing*. New York: Basic Books.

Boud, D. (Ed.). (1988). *Developing student autonomy in learning*.
London: Kogan Page.

Boud, D., Keogh, R., & Walker, D. (Eds.). (1985). *Reflection: Turning experience into learning*. London: Kogan Page.

Boud, D., & Griffin, V. (Eds.). (1987). *Appreciating adults learning:
From the learners' perspective*. London: Kogan Page.

Boyd, E. M. (1981). *Reflection in experiential learning: Case studies on counsellors*. Unpublished doctoral dissertation, Ontario
Institute for Studies in Education.

Brookfield, S. D. (1981). Independent adult learning. *Studies in
Adult Education, 13*, 15–27.

Brookfield, S. D. (1987). *Developing critical thinkers*. San Francisco: Jossey-Bass.

Charnley, A. H., & Jones, H. A. (1981). *The concept of success in
adult literacy*. London: Adult Literacy and Basic Skills Unit.

Conti, G., & Fellenz, R. (1988). Teacher actions that influence
native American learners. In M. Zukas (Ed.), *Papers from the
transatlantic dialogue* (pp. 96–101). Leeds: University of Leeds.

D'Andrea, A. (1985). *Teachers and reflection: A description and analysis of the reflective process which teachers use in their experiential learning.* Unpublished doctoral dissertation, Ontario Institute for Studies in Education.

Danis, C., & Tremblay, N. A. (1988). Autodidactic learning experiences: Questioning established adult learning principles. In H. B. Long & Associates, *Self-directed learning: Application and theory* (pp. 171–198). Athens, GA: Department of Adult Education, University of Georgia.

Denis, M. (1979). *Toward the development of a theory of intuitive learning in adults based on a descriptive analysis.* Unpublished doctoral dissertation, Ontario Institute for Studies in Education.

Edwards, J. (1986). *Working class adult education in Liverpool: A radical approach.* Manchester: Center for Adult and Higher Education, University of Manchester.

Finger, M. (1988). The process of becoming an adult educator. In C. Warren (Ed.), *Proceedings of the Twenty-Ninth Annual Adult Education Research Conference* (pp. 127–132). Calgary: Faculty of Continuing Education, University of Calgary.

Fingeret, A. (1983). Culture shock: Practitioners returning to graduate school. *Lifelong Learning, 6,* 13–14.

Gehrels, C. (1984). *The school principal as learner.* Unpublished doctoral dissertation, Ontario Institute for Studies in Education.

Griffith, G. (1982). *Images of interdependence: Meaning and movement in teaching-learning.* Unpublished doctoral dissertation, Ontario Institute for Studies in Education.

Hutchinson, E., & Hutchinson, E. (1986). *Women returning to learning.* Cambridge, England: National Extension College.

Kolb, D. (1984). *Experiential learning.* Englewood Cliffs: Prentice Hall.

Mezirow, J. (1978). Perspective transformation. *Adult Education, 28,* 100–110.

Millar, C., Morphet, T., & Saddington, T. (1987). Curriculum negotiation in professional adult education. *Journal of Curriculum Studies, 18,* 429–443.

Persico, C. (1988). *Non-traditional technical programs for women: Barriers and facilitators to learning.* Unpublished doctoral dissertation, Department of Higher and Adult Education, Teachers College, Columbia University.

Pratt, D. (1988). Cross-cultural relevance of selected psychological perspectives on learning. In M. Zukas (Ed.), *Papers from the transatlantic dialogue* (pp. 352–357). Leeds: University of Leeds.

Pratt, D. (1989). Culture and learning: A comparison of Western and Chinese conceptions of self and individuality. *Proceedings of the 30th Annual Adult Education Research Conference* (pp. 248–253). Madison: Department of Continuing and Vocational Education, University of Wisconsin-Madison.

Rannells Saul, J. (1989). Women speak about their learning experiences in higher education. *Proceedings of the 30th Annual Adult Education Research Conference* (pp. 278–283). Madison: Department of Continuing and Vocational Education, University of Wisconsin-Madison.

Robinson, J., Saberton, S., & Griffin, V. (1985). *Learning partnerships: Interdependent learning in adult education.* Toronto: Department of Adult Education, Ontario Institute for Studies in Education.

Schön, D. A. (1983). *The reflective practitioner.* New York: Basic Books.

Sheckley, B. (1988). The best and worst classroom learning experiences of adult learners. In M. Zukas (Ed.), *Papers from the transatlantic dialogue* (pp. 381–386). Leeds: University of Leeds.

Spear, G. (1988). Beyond the organizing circumstances: A search for methodology for the study of self-directed learning. In H. B. Long & Associates, *Self-directed learning: Application and theory* (pp. 199–222). Athens, GA: Department of Adult Education, University of Georgia.

Taylor, M. (1979). *Adult learning in an emergent learning group: Toward a theory of learning from the learner's perspective.* Unpublished doctoral dissertation, Ontario Institute for Studies in Education.

Van Tilburg, E., & DuBois, J. E. (1989). Literacy students' perceptions of successful participation in adult education: A cross-cultural approach through expectancy valence. *Proceedings of the 30th Annual Adult Education Research Conference* (pp. 308–313). Madison: Department of Continuing and Vocational Education, University of Wisconsin-Madison.

Whitman, N. A. (1988). *Peer teaching: To teach is to learn twice.* ASHE-ERIC Higher Education Report 4. Washington D.C.: George Washington University.

CHAPTER 3

Individualizing the Teaching and Learning Process
BURTON SISCO
ROGER HIEMSTRA

Nearly all of us have had as role models, teachers who stood before lecterns and provided expert knowledge in the belief that learners will absorb this knowledge and be able to demonstrate this acquisition through some examining procedure. While this modeling may have caused us some anxieties as learners, we often continued similar practices when we became instructors.

For adults, this learner anxiety is magnified because of two circumstances: (a) adults possess diverse levels of education, experience, and expectations, and (b) when given the opportunity most adults prefer to be in charge of their own learning. The problem facing most instructors of adults is finding reliable information that draws upon knowledge about adulthood and then organizing this information into a proven system for helping adults learn. This chapter describes a comprehensive instructional system that addresses this problem in such a way that teaching and learning excellence can occur. The system is the "individualizing instructional process" and is designed to be flexible, practical, and applicable in a variety of settings ranging from training in business and industry to instructing adult nonreaders. It is rooted in much of the educational and training literature produced during the past twenty years which emphasizes the importance of involving adults in deciding what will be learned, how it will be learned, and how the learning will be evaluated. Additionally, the individualizing process is supported by substantial research on self-directed learning and has been tested and retested in actual adult teaching and learning situations.

In this chapter, we briefly describe the origins of the individualizing instructional process and the various assumptions upon which it is based. We then offer a model for organizing instruction in an individualizing manner and discuss some typical activities. We then provide an example of how the individualizing instructional process works in a semester-long course that meets weekly. Finally, we discuss some common issues instructors may face in using the process and how it can lead to greater instructional success. For a more in-depth treatment of the subject, we suggest a look at our recent book titled *Individualizing Instruction: Making Learning Personal, Empowering, and Successful* (1990).

ORIGINS OF THE INDIVIDUALIZING INSTRUCTIONAL PROCESS

For some time now, we have been interested in the teaching and learning of adults. This interest has been fueled by the explosion of writings during the past two decades dealing with the concept of self-direction in learning. Numerous research studies, funded projects, and various published materials have appeared describing the phenomenon and its associated features. Most of this information has emanated from two different but related lines of inquiry started in the 1960s: literature about andragogy (the art and science of teaching adults) and learning projects research. Understanding some of the related features regarding these inquiry lines is useful in talking about the individualization of instruction and why we believe such a process is essential in helping adults learn.

The andragogical model as conceived by Knowles is predicated on four basic assumptions about adults as learners:

1. Their self-concept moves from dependency to independency or self-directedness.

2. They accumulate a reservoir of experiences that can be used as a basis on which to build learning.

3. Their readiness to learn becomes increasingly associated with the developmental tasks of social roles.

4. Their time and curricular perspectives change from postponed to immediacy of application and from subject centeredness to performance centeredness (1980, pp. 44–45).

  Knowles in describing andragogy associated it with a variety of instructional suggestions based on such assumptions and he, too, detailed roles for instructors and discussed ways of helping learners reach their potential. His formative work with andragogy and subsequent analysis of the learning projects research by Tough (1979) and others led to a 1975 publication titled *Self-Directed Learning: A Guide for Learners and Teachers* where he provided a number of inquiry projects and learning resources on the topic.

  Knowles (1975) provided some reasons for why he believed elements of self-direction should be incorporated in the instructional process with adults. One reason was the emerging evidence that people who take initiative in educational activities seem to learn more and learn things better that those who remained what he called "passive." A second reason was that self-direction in learning appears "more in tune with our natural process of psychological development" (Knowles, 1975, p. 14). Knowles asserted that an essential aspect of the maturation process is the development of the ability to take increasing responsibility for life. A third reason was the observation that many new educational innovations such as distance learning, weekend colleges, and correspondence study require that learners bear more responsibility and initiative in their own learning.

  A second line of inquiry parallel and foundational to the andragogical assumptions was the scholarship on self-directed learning that stemmed from the learning projects research. This work was first initiated by Houle (1961) who found that people generally participate in learning activities for goal-oriented, activity-oriented, or learning-oriented reasons. A few years later, Johnstone and Rivera (1965), using a national telephone interview protocol, estimated that at least nine million U.S. adults carried out one or more self-instruction projects annually. Then, in 1971, Tough reported the results of his seminal work on adults' learning projects which indicated, among other things, that most learning is self-planned and occurs outside school or educational settings. A number of subsequent studies have confirmed Tough's original findings.

  In recent years, many authors have written about the teaching and learning of adults. Brookfield (1986, 1987) offers a number of suggestions for facilitating self-directed learning and critical thinking. Knox (1986) describes some teaching strategies with particular emphasis on enhancing various proficiencies in life. Draves (1984) devotes an entire text to the teaching of adults. Long (1983) addresses much of the research on adult teaching and learning. Wlodkowski (1985) provides a number of strategies for understanding and motivating adults to learn. Despite these efforts, the field of adult education has, until recently, lacked a comprehensive resource that capitalizes on adults' nascent need to be self-directing and to have more control of the decisions related to their learning efforts. This void has been filled by our individualizing instructional process.

ASSUMPTIONS OF THE INDIVIDUALIZING INSTRUCTIONAL PROCESS

The individualizing instructional process is predicated on a number of assumptions about the nature of adults and the teaching and learning process. In addition to providing the foundation, these assumptions help guide our actions as instructors. They are consistent with research about adults as learners and emphasize the importance of personal responsibility and action:

1. Adults can and do learn significant things throughout their lives.

2. Educational interventions ought to be organized so that growth and development is the ultimate outcome.

3. The potentiality of humans as learners can only be maximized when there is a deliberate interaction between three elements: the learning process, learning needs and interests, and available instructional resources.

4. When given the opportunity, adults prefer to be in charge of their own learning and actually thrive under such conditions.

5. Adults are capable of self-directed involvement in terms of personal commitment to and responsibility for learning, choice of learning approach, choice of learning resources, and choice of evaluation or validation techniques.

6. The instructor's role is multidimensional, including being a facilitator, manager, resource guide, expert, friend, advocate, authority, coach, and mentor.

7. Empowering learners to take responsibility for their own learning is the ultimate aim of education.

8. Educational interventions ought to promote a negotiated match between the needs of each learner and the needs of the instructor.

9. Teaching and learning excellence is the result of subject matter expertise, careful planning, a good deal of patience and flexibility, and a commitment to helping learners reach their potential.

10. The individualizing instructional process can be utilized in nearly every educational endeavor with commensurate success.

HELPING LEARNERS ASSUME PERSONAL RESPONSIBILITY FOR LEARNING

The individualizing process described in this section is used to help learners, usually meeting in a group setting such as a course or workshop, determine personal learning needs and build appropriate learnings to meet those needs. Personal needs may range from an internal desire to accomplish something altruistic or utilitarian to a desire to meet some external requirement such as a job demand as quickly as possible. Sometimes these needs are known fairly early or can be determined quickly in the instructional process. Other times they are predetermined by a specific content area such as a university credit course or by an employer as in the case of a job training seminar. Still, in other occasions, some learners may need more time and involvement in the instructional process before specific learning needs become clear.

At any event, it is important to recognize that some learners may resent what they perceive as an externally imposed need by an employer or even an instructor. The individualizing instructional process is predicated on the notion that all humans are capable of exercising personal commitment to and responsibility for their own learning. This involves determining what it is they intend to learn, what strategies and resources they will use in accomplishing the learning, and how they will know when the learning is completed.

Some learners will readily embrace such a commitment, while others will need considerable time or guidance from the instructor before they can begin to individualize their own efforts. It has been our experience that most learners thrive under such self-directing conditions and only a very few will actually reject or withdraw from the process.

A Model for Individualizing Instruction

The individualizing instructional process model, shown in Figure 3.1, consists of six specific steps. Each step involves ongoing planning, analyzing, and decision making on the part of the person interested in individualizing the instructional process. The model should be used flexibly as a guide or framework for organizing instruction. If certain elements do not seem to apply to a particular context, then simply modify or remove them; that is one of the strengths of the process.

Step One. Preplanning Activities Prior to the First Group Session. There are many activities to plan and decisions to be made prior to the first meeting of the learning event. Typically, instructors start by developing a rationale statement that describes why the learners should be interested in the learning experience, how it will assist them professionally, how and why it will enable them to develop additional competencies, and what the instructional experience will be like. Other preplanning activities include determining suggested learning competencies and requirements; locating support materials such as books, articles, and audio/video tapes; and securing human resources such as community experts. Some additional preplanning activities include the preparation of a study guide or workbook that includes any necessary syllabus information, learning activity descriptions, bibliographic citations, learning contracts (a tool that helps match individualize learning objectives with individual learner needs), and any special readings or other material.

Step Two. Creating a Positive Learning Environment. Once the learning experience is underway, there are several activities that can help create a good learning environment. These include paying special attention to the physical environment of the room, arranging for bathroom and refreshment breaks, and building a comfortable informal learning situation where participants are encouraged to meet one another. In addition, some attention should be given to how best to introduce the contents of the learning experience, how each participant will become acquainted with one another, and how

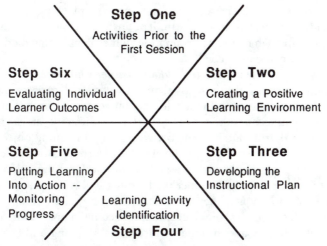

Figure 3.1 Individualizing instructional process model.

the instructor will get to know the participants. We call this the "Three R's": relationship with each other, relationship with the instructor, and relationship with the subject matter.

Step Three. Developing the Instructional Plan. The crucial third step involves discussing such items as suggested learning topics, activities, and objectives. A needs assessment procedure is introduced where participants first individually complete a checklist of potential study topics on the basis of experience and competence. Once completed, small groups are formed for sharing and consensus building. The instructor then uses this information to construct a learning plan that describes the topics to be studied, the sequence, and the instructional techniques.

Step Four. Identifying Learning Activities. This step involves the identification of various learning activities, techniques, and approaches that participants might use in developing and implementing their learning plans. We use learning contracts as a means for such self-directed planning. Typically, learning activities take many forms, are dependent upon the competency needs of each individual learner, and are negotiated between the instructor and learner.

Step Five. Putting Learning Into Action—Monitoring Progress. Once the learning plan has been established, the next step is putting it into action and monitoring progress. This is accomplished through a variety of techniques including lectures, case studies, small and large group discussions, simulations, role playing, field visits, individual projects, and so forth. The instructor monitors learner progress through formative evaluations which enable plan modifications to be made as needed.

Step Six. Evaluating Individual Learner Outcomes. The sixth and final step of the individualzing instructional process model consists of evaluating individual learner outcomes. Because all learners are unique and their experiential base different, it is vitally important that a match occur between desired learning objectives and subject mastery. Through the use of the learning contract, learners are able to articulate what it is they want to learn, how they will learn it, what form or product the learning will result in, and how they will know when they have acquired the desired competency level. In this case, the role of evaluation becomes a process of development, mastery, and stimulator for critical thinking and learning rather than the more usual form of punishment or reward.

Throughout the six-step process, the underlying intent is to promote good educational practice through the recognition of individual differences, experiences, and learning needs. By capitalizing upon the resident expertise so common in older, more mature learners, instructors can create the conditions for good learning to occur. We believe that optimum learning is the result of careful planning between the instructor and individual learners. The individualizing process is designed to enable this to occur.

The ultimate challenge for any instructor is finding ways of bringing the best out in learners. Content mastery is important as is the process that enables mastery to occur. Understanding the instructional process, helping learners realize their potential, being flexible and supportive when the need arises, and varying one's teaching methods so that active learning is the result, are all ingredients for instructional success. In the next section, we will illustrate how the individualizing instructional process can be used in a typical teaching and learning situation.

APPLYING THE INDIVIDUALIZING INSTRUCTIONAL PROCESS: A TYPICAL EXAMPLE

The individualizing process can be used in nearly every adult teaching and learning situation with accompanying success. For example, the process has been used in training workshops, intensive summer courses, conference presentations, weekend courses, laboratory based courses, and the like. Since it would be impossible to describe how the process works in each particular context, we have chosen to illustrate its uses in a typical semester-long course that meets weekly. Regardless of setting, the basic rudiments of the individualizing process hold and thus should be transferable. If certain modifications are necessary, that is okay since it is designed to be flexible.

The individualizing process begins with considerable preplanning and design work, such as locating relevant text materials and learning resources. A workbook of materials is organized containing a syllabus, suggested course requirements, and various supplemental materials such as bibliographic suggestions, a glossary of terms, and guides for executing the learning activities. The workbook also contains material about self-directed learning, our views about teaching and learning and how we intend to use the individualizing instructional process, and the learners' potential for assuming greater responsibility for their own learning. For learners seeking more structure and direction, we provide a suggested list of learning objectives as well as resources and activities usually employed to achieve satisfactory competence in terms of course content.

The next activity involves arriving before the first session early enough so the physical space can be made more comfortable and conducive to learning. This typically involves rearranging chairs, attending to the room's temperature, and preparing refreshments such as coffee or tea.

As the participants arrive, we often greet each person individually and indicate how nice it is to have them with us. We then provide some opening remarks about the course, the teaching and learning process we will use, and a few brief comments about the purpose of the course. We then ask participants to turn to their neighbor or count off in twos and work in dyads. We give them an interview sheet and then have them spend about fifteen minutes conversing so they can introduce their dyadic partner to the rest of the group. This enables two people to quickly become acquainted and for others in the group to learn something about each participant through subsequent introductions.

Following the introduction exercise and a question and answer period about course materials and requirements, we typically provide a brief ten minute break for learners to register and purchase course materials. Then, we introduce and carry out both an individual and a group needs assessment activity. This involves a short instructor generated instrument usually consisting of up to fifteen topics that are typically covered in the course. We ask learners to rank the topics according to four self-rating categories, "don't know," "low competence," "medium competence," and "high competence." The learners are also asked to add any topics not indicated on the instrument that they believe would be appropriate. This helps us "personalize" the learning experience by taking into account the learners' expertise, competency levels, and perceived needs beyond those we identified. The learners then move into small groups of four or five and discuss their individual ratings and see if they can come to some consensus about which topics should be given a high priority and which a low priority. Finally, we ask each small group to report their rankings to the reassembled large group. Before concluding the first session, we usually describe learning contracts, and make some general remarks about the course content. We encourage any learner who may have some trepidation about the individualizing approach to talk to us after class. If anyone does express some confusion or concerns, usually we can provide satisfactory clarification so they can proceed comfortably.

The next week is usually spent reviewing the needs assessment information and developing a tentative course plan which lays out a weekly schedule of learning experiences, suggests appropriate learning goals and objectives, describes various learning resources, and explicates any required course deadlines. Every attempt is made to ensure that the weekly schedule is flexible and that there is adequate "flex time" so that certain topics can be explored in depth as needs and interests dictate.

During the second class meeting, we present the tentative course plan to the group and discuss its content. We emphasize that the plan is tentative and reflective of the group's needs and competency levels, not ours. At this point, we ask for any modifications or adjustments and after some discussion, put the tentative plan into final form. We then indicate to the group that we will bring a finalized course plan during our next meeting. Our experience suggests that most learners will be very comfortable with this process and plan of action since it reflects their needs and interests. In a few cases, however, some learners may still disagree with portions of the plan. If this occurs, we usually ask such learners to meet with one or both of us outside of class where we will negotiate some alternative means of completing the course. There have been a few occasions where no acceptable plan could be negotiated and a learner subsequently dropped the course. We hasten to add, however, that this occurs very rarely. The remainder of the second session typically involves leading some learning activities that reflect some command and immediate needs.

During the third class meeting, we report back to the group the final class plan and encourage participants to start developing personal learning contracts that emphasize ways of meeting their individual needs. Here the essence of the individualizing instructional process is at work. Learning contracts typically consist of information about what each participant intends to learn, what resources and the strategies will be used, what form the learning will be presented in as evidence of accomplishment, how the evidence will be evaluated or validated which demonstrates mastery, and an expected time frame for completing the various activities (Knowles, 1986). We ask each participant to turn in a tentative contract within the next six to eight weeks so that we can provide feedback regarding how complete and realistic the plan is for completing course requirements. We also emphasize that learning contracts may be renegotiated at any time up to the end of the course depending upon individual needs or changes in competency desires.

During the remainder of the course, our role begins to parallel traditional instruction in many ways with one notable exception; considerable feedback is given to participants along the way as a means of monitoring progress and ensuring that we are on target in meeting the desired proficiencies of the group. We use a variety of instructional techniques aimed at keeping interest high both for us and for the learners. These include lecturing, small and large group discussion, debates, case study analysis, and role playing. We also use mediated resources and outside experts as well as various gaming and simulation activities. In addition, we provide one-on-one communication to learners in the form of written feedback and individual appointments, help in securing needed learning resources, and ongoing assessment of any class assignments turned in. We also encourage participants to work with each other outside of class through study groups or team efforts on various learning activities.

We use a number of evaluation techniques. The first effort involves formative evaluation procedures as the learning experience unfolds. Here, special attention is paid to such things as nonverbal body and facial communications, employing a written midterm evaluation of us and the course, occasionally soliciting written feedback on certain aspects of the course, and encouraging individual appointments outside of class if problems emerge. Another technique, given at the end of the course, is an instructor rating form to check on how well each of us has facilitated self-directed learning. The third technique is another instrument used at the end of the course which evaluates the process used, content covered, and resources employed during the learning experience. In all cases, we tell participants not to provide their names unless they want to; we have found that most learners are more candid in their evaluations if anonymity is assured, although some will choose to provide their names. It has also been our experience that most learners take these evaluation activities very seriously, thus giving us the kind of feedback needed to improve our own teaching and the individualizing instructional process. We also regularly ask learners how they are coming on their learning plans and in their various efforts at evaluating or validating their progress.

As noted earlier, the individualizing process has been employed with accompanying success in nearly every adult education context imaginable. In some cases, instructors may be bound by certain constraints which limit the degree to which the process can be fully implemented. For example in business and industry, employers often dictate what employees will learn, when they will learn it, and under what conditions. In short, there is less room for learners to take responsibility for their own learning since it has been externally imposed on them.

We readily admit that this does occur and suggest that the instructor in such a situation be open and candid with the learners about the existing constraints. At the same time, aspects of the individualizing process can be used in such a learning setting regardless of limitations, such as emphasizing multiple routes for competency mastery, acknowledging and utilizing the resident expertise in each employee, and using a variety of instructional techniques. Through careful planning and imagination, the individualizing process can be successfully employed without compromising the overall intent of helping learners reach their potential.

CONCERNS IN USING THE INDIVIDUALIZING PROCESS

Most instructors teach the way they were taught. This usally means assuming an authority position where all decisions about a particular teaching and learning event rest with the instructor. While this approach certainly has some value for situations requiring a high degree of control and structure, such as the training setting described above, our experience with adult learners suggests an individualizing approach is much more effective since it recognizes and builds upon learners' innate capacities for self-direction. The problem is that nearly everywhere we turn, we see instructors controlling all aspects of the teaching and learning process. It is no wonder many people who become involved with instructing conclude that this must be the best way to teach. In our experience, the individualizing process is a viable alternative approach. However, we acknowledge there may be certain probems for instructors wishing to incorporate rudiments of the process into their teaching. As a way of helping them deal with some of these issues, we discuss several means for coping.

One issue that many instructors may face in using the individualizing approach is being perceived by certain learners as too loose and permissive. This should not be too surprising, however, since most learners have been accustomed to a more teacher-directed approach. In addition, some learners naturally resist change more than others and thus find anything new or different a challenge to their well-being.

To deal with this situation and help those individuals more likely to resist change, we suggest instructors try the following. First, be aware that some learners are going to perceive the instructor's role in a conventional or teacher-directed manner. This means that the instructor will be expected to tell the learners exactly what it is they will learn, how they will learn, and how they will be evaluated. We suggest instructors confront this expectation immediately during the first encounter with participants. Tell them something about yourself and your feelings regarding the role of education in life. Briefly describe some of the pertinent findings from the self-directed learning literature which suggests that most adults, when given the opportunity, prefer to be in charge of their own learning. Discuss how this has impacted on your own teaching to a point where you organize it differently from what they have experi-

enced before. Tell them about the individualizing process, noting
how it emphasizes shared responsibility for teaching and learning.
Describe how your role will sometimes be more traditional as a
content-transmitter, other times as a manager of resources, and still
other times as a facilitator of learning. Stress your commitment to
helping learners meet their own needs and interests, highlighting
that this may initially cause some trepidation since learners are
typically not given a say in the teaching and learning process. Ask
any learners present in the classroom who have already been exposed to the individualizing process to give a testimonial about such
experiences. Finally, give lots of support and encouragement while
new learners become more "comfortable" with the individualizing
process.

Second, try the process or elements of the process you are
interested in at least three times. We believe this is essential in order to
weigh the relative merits of the individualizing process and to evaluate it thoroughly. The reason for this is because the first time you use
it, the process will be new to both you and the learners. The second
time it will be new to the learners but not yourself, and the third time,
it will be routine enough so that you can critically evaluate the process and its impact. Again, those learners who have already experienced the process can serve as role models for new participants.

Another issue some instructors encounter is colleagues' questions about the validity of the individualizing instructional process.
Frankly speaking, some colleagues are threatened by the notion of
giving learners a role in the teaching and learning process. They
often possess the traditional views noted above about what an instructor should and should not do. Rather than be threatened by
this reaction, we suggest the best defense is offense. We have found
that most colleagues are at least open to sharing their views of
instruction. You can do the same but we recommend doing so in a
neutral location over coffee or tea. There, you can share your views
of instruction much as you would when first introducing the individualizing process to a group of new learners. While you may not
convince everyone, at the very least they will have a more informed
idea of what you are attempting to do instructionally.

Another useful technique is to invite colleagues to view your
classes and evaluate them accordingly. Try to find a mutually conducive time for such observations and emphasize your desire to receive
honest feedback about your instructional efforts. We have found

that being open to evaluation usually at least wins some respect and helps colleagues understand the value of the individualizing process.

There may also be certain institutional policies or procedures that interfere with your using the individualizing process. For example, certain institutions require the use of a standardized syllabus format. If this is the case, go ahead and follow the prescribed format but provide additional information relevant to the individualizing process through attachments or appendices. We have found that this type of compromise usually results in satisfying the needs of both parties.

One issue that confronts many instructors is how much time is needed to fully implement the individualizing process. This varies depending upon how much preplanning has been done and the instructor's willingness to experiment with the instructional process. As a rule of thumb, it usually takes at least three offerings before the process is completely in place. For example, when beginning a new course or workshop, we typically plan on offering the experience three times before the individualizing process is totally activated. The reasons for this are many and generally revolve around the time it takes to develop a rationale for the learning experience, determine suggested learning requirements and competencies, identify necessary support materials, and secure needed learning resources such as community experts.

One final issue that instructors may face in using the individualizing process is how comfortable they feel in moving to a more personalized instructional form. Our experience suggests that the individualizing process may be easier for beginning instructors to assimilate than their more experienced counterparts. Novice instructors can quickly recall their experiences as learners and remember their feelings of frustration and anxiety. They are also typically less set in their views of instruction and more open or eager to learn ways of improving their instructional approach. This phenomenon may seem ironic since professional experience is often viewed positively, but our personal experiences confirm such observations.

SUCCESS WITH THE INDIVIDUALIZING PROCESS

The individualizing instructional process boasts a number of benefits that can contribute to greater success in teaching adults. Perhaps the greatest benefit is the notable joy you will derive from teaching and the corresponding satisfaction the learners will derive from learning. We have repeatedly observed this reaction and are confident in saying that the individualizing process is a major part of the reason.

But there are other advantages. One is how much easier and more pleasurable you will find the teaching and learning experience. This is because the individualizing process emphasizes flexibility, adaptability, cooperative learning, and personal responsibility for learning which reduces the anxiety ever present in traditional pedagogy. It is common to find learners thriving in the individualizing process, motivated to engage deeply and critically in working toward their potential. As a matter of fact, we have frequently needed to help learners set realistic goals in their learning contracts once they become really excited about a topic.

Another benefit comes from the satisfaction you and the learners will derive in learning together. In our view, satisfied learners are motivated learners and to the extent you create this kind of enthusiasm, all the better. The old adage of leading a horse to water may be particularly fitting here: your role as an instructor isn't to make the horse drink, rather it is making the horse thirsty. And so it is with motivated learners; they are ever thirsty for more.

A final benefit we would note here comes from the joy you will feel in knowing that learners are responding to a learning system designed for them. Indeed, some may balk when first exposed to the individualizing process and this may temper your enthusiasm for it, too. But once the learners understand the process and start experiencing the freedom of choice permitted, they will respond in an infectious way. This infection will spread to a point where you will know the harmony of teaching and learning together.

CONCLUSION

The purpose of this chapter was to describe a comprehensive instructional system—the individualizing instructional process—for teaching adults. The origins of the process were briefly examined as were the various assumptions upon which it is based. We then introduced a six-step model depicting the various elements of the process and discussed how adult instructors can use it to more effectively organize their own teaching efforts. We also provided an illustration of how the individualizing process works in a typical semester-long course meeting weekly. We concluded the chapter by noting some common issues instructors may face in using the individualizing process and suggested some of the potential benefits.

The teaching of adults is one of the most rewarding experiences in life. The joy of watching mature individuals grow and develop is something to which most adult instructors can relate. Yet, it can be made even more satisfying once the rudiments of adulthood and instruction are integrated. It is hoped that this chapter shed some light on how this can be accomplished.

REFERENCES

Brookfield, S. D. (1986). *Understanding and facilitating adult learning*. San Francisco: Jossey-Bass.

Brookfield, S. D. (1987). *Developing critical thinkers*. San Francisco: Jossey-Bass.

Draves, W. A. (1984). *How to teach adults*. Manhattan, KS: The Learning Resources Network.

Hiemstra, R., & Sisco, B. (1990). *Individualizing instruction: Making learning personal, empowering, and successful*. San Francisco: Jossey-Bass.

Houle, C. O. (1961). *The inquiring mind*. Madison, WI: The University of Wisconsin Press.

Johnstone, J., & Rivera, R. (1965). *Volunteers for learning: A study of the educational pursuits of American adults*. Chicago: Aldine.

Knowles, M. S. (1975). *Self-directed learning*. New York: Association Press.

Knowles, M. S. (1980). *The modern practice of adult education* (revised and updated). New York: Cambridge.

Knowles, M. S. (1986). *Using learning contracts*. San Francisco: Jossey-Bass.

Knox, A. B. (1986). *Helping adults learn*. San Francisco: Jossey-Bass.

Long, H. B. (1983). *Adult learning: Research and practice*. New York: Cambridge.

Tough, A. M. (1979). *The adult's learning projects*. Austin, TX: Learning Concepts.

Wlodkowski, R. J. (1985). *Enhancing adult motivation to learn*. San Francisco: Jossey-Bass.

CHAPTER 4

Paradigms for Critically Reflective Teaching and Learning

VICTORIA J. MARSICK
KAREN E. WATKINS

As teachers and facilitators, it is easy to become enamored of method. But in instruction, method is highly influenced by the teacher's perceptions and beliefs. The teachers' use of learning methods is highly colored by the lens through which they view themselves, their work, and their world. In this chapter, various metaphors are used as a lens to explore the adult learning transactional process. These different lenses illustrate a shift in paradigms, that is, a "view of the world—a *Weltanschauung*—that reflects our most basic beliefs and assumptions about the human condition, whether or not there is any such thing as 'sin,' what is real, what is true, what is beautiful, and what is the nature of things" (Lincoln, 1985, p. 29). Scholars and practitioners in many disciplines are talking about paradigm shifts because of rapidly changing conditions that call for new conceptual frameworks by which to understand our world, both as lay persons and as professionals. One of the benefits of rapidly changing conditions is that people become aware of rules, long taken for granted, by which they make sense of their world and begin to question whether or not these traditional ways of doing things produce the results they want to achieve.

In this chapter, metaphors are used to examine some of the paradigms that have governed views of learning and to explore alternative views that might better suit the adult learning transactional process. The chapter begins with a discussion of three metaphors for understanding the paradigm shift—that of the machine, the organic system, and the brain—and the implications these metaphors might have for understanding transactional learning and the role of the teacher or facilitator. This is followed by a discussion of critically reflective learning, which is compatible with the brain metaphor and transactional learning. Critically reflective learning is found in three related approaches, each of which will be highlighted through examples of strategies used to enhance practice: action science, reflection-in-action, and action learning. Finally, the chapter concludes with a look at the skills needed to be an effective facilitator of critically reflective learning.

PARADIGM SHIFTS AND LEARNING

This chapter is based on previous works by the co-authors in which metaphors have been used to interpret the shift taking place toward an information society and its impact upon understanding and facilitating learning (Marsick & Watkins, 1990; Marsick, 1987; Watkins, 1989). Drawing from the works of Mitroff (1983) and Morgan (1986), metaphors can be used to illustrate three ways of looking at learning: that of the machine, the organic system, and the brain.

The Machine, the System, and the Brain Metaphors

The Machine. It is not uncommon to find people who explain social institutions in terms of a machine. Using this metaphor, one can envisage people who interact with one another in terms of well-orchestrated parts of a whole. This does not necessarily imply a cold, inhuman perspective. However, for the machine to function effectively in different social settings, people must learn and enact a set of skills that enable them, in their capacity in the machine, to mesh with other people in their roles in relationship to a greater whole.

The machine metaphor can be used, for example, to describe learning in a classroom. The teacher is expected to know and do certain things. The learners are expected to read, do homework, ask and answer questions. The administrators are expected to ensure that the institution functions smoothly so that classes can be held. The support staff must make sure that supplies are in place, mail processed, and the building kept clean and in good repair. The machine metaphor can as easily be used to describe a social gathering. A host and/or hostess makes certain arrangements for a formal party. Guests, in turn, arrive on time, dress as expected, are on their best behavior, and function in certain social roles vis-à-vis one another. Organizations, characterized by the machine metaphor, place a premium on logic and rationality, linear cause-effect relationships, clear demarcation of responsibilities, hierarchical control, and forged unification of the movement of parts into a whole which minimizes duplication and overlap. Historically, the machine metaphor fits with the industrial revolution, wih the Weberian bureaucratic ideal, and with many of the values of science during that period.

The System. While the machine metaphor is still useful and accurate for many circumstances, the systems metaphor is increasingly a more appropriate description of many social interactions. The systems metaphor derives from the human body in which various functions and parts interact organically. The health of one part of the system is intricately tied to the health of another part. If one part of the body is ill, it will inevitably affect other parts of the body. A mobile is another example of a system; if you tug at one part of the mobile, it will automatically interfere with the balance of the entire system. A systems model is usually described in terms of inputs, processes, outputs, and feedback systems. Systems are seen as interacting units; not only do the parts of the human body interact internally, but they are affected by external pressures from the larger system in which the person functions.

Looking at the classroom as a system, learning is not just what teachers do to learners and what learners do for themselves, but an interaction among all the persons involved. In this model, the process of interaction become central to learning. Unlike in the machine metaphor, it is not enough for each person to carry out a preplanned role. As people bounce ideas off one another, learning becomes a mutual transaction that often moves in unanticipated directions. Moreover, what happens in the classroom may alter the kind of support that needs to be provided by administrators or support staff, or vice versa. The systems metaphor would also result in a different kind of social gathering. While courtesies might still be involved among the host or hostess and guests, the evening may begin with polite conversation but, at the urging of guests, change into an opportunity for singing along with a talented guitarist who happened to accompany one of the guests. The systems model has been highly useful in organizational change because people can tinker with the various parts of the interbalanced organization to get different results. By increasing the number and quality of educational inputs, improving the teaching and learning processes which produce the outputs, or by drawing resources more effectively from the environment or learning context, we can alter the cost and effectiveness of our learning outputs (Watkins, 1989).

The Brain. A third metaphor for understanding social settings is that of the brain, the center of intelligence, through which information is both processed and simultaneously evaluated, so that, if something is going wrong, a new course of action can be developed. This metaphor is useful for understanding social settings today, in part, because of the speed of communications and what seems to be an enhanced pace of action. The metaphor of the brain is different from the systems model, even though both are organic, because the emphasis is on information processing and self-correcting, intelligent direction of activity. Moreover, if one part of the brain is damaged, another part of the brain can sometimes develop the capacity to substitute for the the damaged part, thus preserving the health of the entire organism. Even though the brain's component parts are specialized, numerous connective elements create a "pattern of rich connectivity . . . (that) allows simultaneous processing of information in different parts of the brain . . . and an amazing capacity to be aware of what is going on elsewhere" (Morgan, 1986, p. 96).

Applying the brain metaphor to classrooms, we see learning interactions that go beyond the simpler concept that the teacher and learners mutually affect one another. In this classroom, a higher order interaction takes place whereby information is being simultaneously processed and critically evaluated by all the members of the group. While the teacher retains responsibility for making this kind of interaction happen, other learners are equally important and can, at times, develop and carry out a leadership role as the teacher steps back to let this capacity emerge. In a brain-like classroom, the teacher encourages members of the class to examine the teacher's thinking in the same way they are asked to examine their own. In other words, the unit functions like a community of learners all of whom share responsibility for learning from whatever takes place in the classroom. This community could extend, at times, to other people in the institution that have an impact on learning. For example, if support staff were calling a strike, they might come to class-rooms to examine their point of view with the teacher and learners. Administrators might engage the teacher and learners in a dialogue around aspects of the institution that affect the learner, such as policies about the library, computer rooms, or other support facili-ties. The key idea here is that learning how to learn is a constant parallel curriculum to whatever else is being learned.

The brain metaphor can be used to describe social gatherings as well. In the previous example, people capitalized upon the avail-ability of a guitarist and the interest of the guests. A brain-like social gathering might be one in which the guests were expected to come and create their own entertainment. The host or hostess would make arrangements for this to happen, but would then be part of a group making joint decisions about the social setting, mutually exploring their separate musical meanings as well as reflecting on what makes meaning in music and in social situations. In a class-room which functioned like a brain, learners would be encouraged to learn both specialized knowledge and skills, but also to develop an overall understanding of the nature of the teaching and learning process so that they can design their own learning throughout their lives. Working separately, few learners have a broad enough picture of the nature of the learning process to be able to develop complex solutions to complex problems. Yet, by forming a learning commu-nity, individuals would be encouraged to share what they know that could contribute to solving problems, thereby increasing exponen-tially the brain power that is being used to address these problems. Brain-like classrooms would encourage shared power and participa-tion in decision making between teachers and learners, and joint efforts to identify problems before they occur because these pro-cesses allow learning to occur continuously.

Summary. Social settings can be described in terms of three metaphors: that of the machine, the organic system, and the brain. Learning can be described using one or more of these metaphors. For example, a teacher can function in a machine-like mode by helping students learn and practice certain predefined blocks of knowledge and skill. The teacher is the expert in this capacity, takes the leadership role in the learning proess, and ensures mastery of whatever topic is being studied. Learners are not expected to con-tribute to the shaping of goals or to one another's development.

Alternatively, the teacher can recognize that learners belong to larger, more complex systems. Learners are helped to analyze their role in these systems and plan for the best way to satisfy their learning needs. The learners take initiative for their learning in the systems framework. The teacher helps the learners achieve their goals. The class is, in itself, a system; the needs of various persons are balanced to meet as many of its members' needs as possible and people are drawn upon as resources in one another's learning.

Finally, the teacher can look at learning as a self-monitoring, self-correcting process similar to that of the brain. The teacher in this model is more of an equal to the learners in a process of joint discovery although everyone is presumed to also have specialized knowledge and is expected to share it. The teacher is skilled in helping people think in order to mutually examine and challenge beliefs, ideas, and practices. Individuals take responsibility for their learning, as in the systems model, but learning cannot be effective if the individual does not also seek the help of others in the process because of the blind spots, habitual responses, and taken-for-granted beliefs that color one's view of the world. The class becomes involved in a collaborative inquiry that may change the way in which people define a situation and seek solutions to a problem.

These three metaphors for learning are not necessarily mutually exclusive since each is valuable for different purposes, and in some cases, one approach builds upon the other. The machine metaphor is useful when there is clearly one right answer or set of procedures which learners must master. The systems metaphor is useful when there is no right answer, one needs to look at the interacting parts of a whole, and people are capable of meeting many of their own needs, given help in planning and resources. The brain metaphor is useful when people, as they interact together in groups, must become self-monitoring learning communities because there are not clear, unambiguous answers to problems or even agreement about the nature of the problem.

CRITICALLY REFLECTIVE LEARNING

While it is hard to fully describe and prescribe the kind of learning that takes place when using the brain metaphor, we think one of its key features is critically reflective learning. Brookfield (1987) reviews multiple perspectives on critical thinking which variously emphasize logical reasoning, judgment, reflection, the making of meaning, emancipation from sociocultural forces that shape one's self-image and actions, or dialectical thinking. He then defines critical thinking in terms of the following components: identifying and challenging assumptions, challenging the importance of context, imagining and exploring alternatives, and reflective skepticism.

Brookfield discusses tools and techniques to enhance critical thinking, focusing primarily on the individual. Our approach to critically reflective learning involves critical thinking as well, but we place the dynamics of such thinking more in the context of interpersonal interaction in social settings, both natural and created, for the purpose of learning.

Action Science

Argyris and Schön, separately and together, have developed a theory of action science that also emphasizes critically reflective thinking (Argyris & Schön, 1974, 1978; Argyris, Putnam & Smith, 1985; Schön, 1983, 1987). However, it is known less as a theory of critical thinking, even though Brookfield's (1987) descriptors would also be true of the processes involved in action science, than as a theory of action, intervention, or change. Argyris and Schön are also more concerned than is Brookfield with the way in which individual actions are influenced by people's perceptions of the behavioral worlds in which they live and work. People frequently act on perceptions, expectations, and judgments which they attribute to other people, often unconsciously. These perceptions may be linked to their past experience and personalities, but they are also frequently linked to social and organizational norms about how they think they should act in the situation. Argyris (1970) stresses that despite the interdependencies that develop between the client system and the intervenor, the intervenor should focus on how to maintain or increase the autonomy of the client system. The client, says Argyris, must be the system as a whole regardless of where one initially begins to work. Interventions must, over time, provide all members with opportunities to enhance their competence and effectiveness. In the teaching and learning context this would mean that we would need to view the teacher and the learners in their entire context—both in terms of the educational context, but also the personal context in which each must ultimately be effective.

Argyris and Schön begin with the notion that people do not

deliberately set out to create error, yet error happens. When people make mistakes, they can try out alternative solutions without questioning the basic way in which they have framed the problem; or they can question underlying beliefs, assumptions, and values that produce error because the problem was not properly framed. Argyris and Schön call this difference single- versus double-loop learning, using a concept developed by Ashby (1952), who also illustrated the concept with the example of a thermostat. Corrections made by a thermostat to keep the temperature at a pre-set level involve single-loop learning, whereas asking questions about why the temperature was set at the level in the first place involves double-loop learning. For people to learn in a double-loop fashion, they must develop certain skills in making explicit the reasoning that often leads them to the actions they take. To do this, they must be part of a learning community in which it is possible to publicly inquire into and test one's hypotheses and beliefs in an atmosphere of openness, personal ownership of one's actions, and commitment to change.

　　Double-loop learning is difficult to engage in by oneself because it involves the identification and examination of hidden values that govern action. These hidden values govern what Argyris and Schön (1974) call theories-in-use, that is, descriptions someone could develop of how people think and act under different circumstances by observing their behavior. People are seldom conscious of their theories-in-use. If asked to explain their behavior, they usually respond with espoused theories that they would like to follow but cannot actually reproduce. People learn in action science by examining case studies of situations that did not end as they would like, but were in some way problematic or surprising. With the help of others, they try to reconstruct the reasoning that is often implicit and unexpressed that leads them to speak or act as they do.

　　An Example. The teaching and learning strategies of human resource developers can be illustrated in a case developed by a trainer called the Kingsley case that is quite typical of dilemmas that teachers face when learners have not come to a class of their own accord. In this case, a female trainer interacts with a doctor during the third day of a three day training session, the purpose of which is to teach interpersonal skills to forty medical professionals. The doctor (Kingsley), who has been sitting in the back of the room doing his own work since the training began, refuses to participate in an exercise on behavioral styles and objects to the use of the instrument which he calls "garbage pop psychology." The trainer is annoyed and frustrated, but tries to answer him rationally by explaining that she has data in her office to validate the instrument and tries to bargain with him for his cooperation by agreeing to send the data if he agrees to participate. The doctor flatly refuses and tells her he does not think he could learn anything from her that he hadn't learned in medical school. This pushes the trainer to the point of tears which she holds back as she tells him he is responsible for his own learning and that "it's no skin off my nose if you don't learn anything."

This case is an illustration of what Argyris and Schön suggest people typically do when they create errors out of a lack of awareness of the underlying values that push them to be ineffective by the standards of effectiveness which they themselves espouse. In this case, the trainer wanted to be considered competent and professional, but her interaction with the doctor made her look incompetent and unprofessional. Moreover, the interaction is itself an illustration of poor communication in a workshop where the trainer is supposed to be teaching effective communication skills. The trainer became defensive which made it difficult for her and the doctor to learn from the situation. For example, the doctor could have been legitimately questioning the validity of this instrument, while instead the trainer assumed he was questioning her competence. The trainer's implicit belief appeared to be that whenever a learner challenged her actions, she was afraid that she would lose control and credibility, so she used humor or sarcasm, bargaining, and aggressive confrontation to control the learner, which guaranteed that she would lose control and credibility.

In order to clarify the causal reasoning which produces error on the part of the teacher/trainer, a map of the incident is developed. Mapping is a technique used by Argyris and Schön which identifies and links the underlying values of the person, the action strategies observed that follow from this value, and the possible unintended consequences or consequences for learning. A map of this incident would show that the trainer was using self-protective strategies in this incident. Her desire to retain control to ensure learning (her value) led her to design activities for learners without their input, to ignore challenges to the design, and to use interpersonal control strategies to manage the learners (her action strategies). This in turn led to little learning or possibly even to the unintended learning by the participants that it was more important to behave than to learn (the consequences). What is especially powerful about the action science technique of mapping is the way in which it makes visible to the teacher/trainer in this case the hidden curriculum which both teachers and learners have long felt to be in existence, but which neither has been able to explicitly observe and own as a product of their individual actions.

An alternative map in action science is developed from the model of double-loop learning which calls for a reflective over a self-protective stance. These maps are developed to encourage individuals to change their practices so the hidden curriculum is more consistent with their values regarding the nature of effective teaching and learning. An alternative map which might allow for more reflection on the part of the trainer and the participants would call for all to inquire into the situation as a learning community. This would mean that the trainer would have to relax her defenses and share control of the learning process (in other words, change her value of control to one of learning). This might lead the trainer to jointly design learning experiences and explore challenges to her design as hypotheses to be tested and as potentially helpful alternatives. Specifically, in this instance, the trainer might explore with the group the importance of validity in instruments and her shared concern that the activities of the training session be valid. All might inquire into what makes for a valid, effective training/learning situation. The consequences might be a greater degree of learning for everyone concerned as well as shared responsibility for the process.

Strategies to Enhance Practice. It takes time to develop the kinds of skills that action scientists use in their practice. However, some simple tools can be used by teachers to facilitate critically reflective learning, in particular, language analysis, an awareness of one's "left hand column" of unexpressed thoughts and feelings, and use of the ladder of inference. Argyris and Schön point out that people frequently make assumptions, judgments, and attributions in talking with others without illustrating these assertions with directly observable data. In the Kingsley case, for example, the trainer says at one point, "Come on, Kingsley, lighten up. You might accidentally learn something." Her judgment is that Kingsley does not expect to learn. Alternatively, she could have illustrated this opinion and inquired whether or not the attribution she had made about Kingsley was correct, as for example in the following possible statement:

> Kingsley, in the past two days you have consistently sat at the back of the room and done your own work rather than participate in various training activities. This leads me to believe that you do not expect to learn in this workshop. Am I correct in this assumption?

The trainer also could have become more aware of and perhaps shared material in her "left hand column," that is, those things that she was thinking or feeling but did not express. She could have also asked others in the class what they were thinking or feeling, but did not share. By keeping this material secret, she could not examine the assumptions and values on which she was acting. It is true that, by doing this, she would be taking a risk and might also open up feelings that were quite powerful for her. But, dealing with emotions is a key component of being able to teach in a critically reflective manner. Emotions are indicators of powerful beliefs and values that have often remained tacit and could be holding one back from more effective actions. The ability to help learners learn in potentially potent emotional situations is a sign of expert practice.

Finally, teachers could use the ladder of inference as a tool for examining theories-in-use. The ladder of inference, as Argyris and Schön (1974, 1978) describe it, consists of various levels of abstraction from the directly observable data in a situation to inferred meanings imposed upon this data to even more generalized theories which we apply to future situations. Teachers and learners can help one another construct ladders of inference for their actions similar to those identified in Figure 4.1 for the trainer and for Kingsley concerning their interpretations of Kingsley's questions about the validity and reliability of the instrument being used.

Reflection-in-Action

Central to action science, then, and to critically reflective learning in social situations through the brain metaphor are elements similar to those identified by Brookfield (1987)—identifying and challenging assumptions, challenging the importance of context, imagining and exploring alternatives, and reflective skepticism. Critically reflective learning in action science as used by Argyris, Putnam, Smith (1985), however, is a method oriented to

Kingsley's Ladder of Inference

3 Pop psychologists use invalid instruments which insult my intelligence and my medical training.
2 Without validation, the results of this instrument will be meaningless pop psychology.
1 Is this instrument valid and reliable?

The Trainer's Ladder of Inference

3 Participants who question my methods must be controlled or handled if I am to be credible and professional.
2 He's questioning my credibility and professionalism.
1 Is this instrument valid and reliable?

An Alternative Ladder of Inference

3 It is my professional responsibility to use only those reliable instruments I am trained to use and interpret and participants have a right to be concerned about this issue.
2 The participant wants to be assured that I have chosen a "safe" instrument.
1 Is this instrument valid and reliable?

Source: K. E. Watkins
Figure 4.1 *Possible ladders of inference in the Kingsley case.*

difficult interpersonal interactions that are part of a system or culture of learning or nonlearning.

Schön (1983, 1987), using the same perspective, focuses less on interpersonal interaction and more on professional artistry. He uses the tools of action science to explore the knowing-in-action of professionals as they make sense of new situations. Knowing-in-action is the know-how that people reveal in their intelligent action, but which is typically unexpressed and often difficult to make verbally explicit. Professionals have a repertoire of knowledge and experience, which they might call rules, on which they draw when they encounter a new situation. Professionals look for similarities between the situation and their rules to make judgments about action needed. When the situation and the rules do not fit exactly as desired, the professional must experiment with alternative courses of actions. Often this experimentation takes place without much conscious thought, and as Weick (1983) suggests with respect to managers, thinking and acting may take place simultaneously.

Schön (1983) suggests that professionals engage in conversations with a situation, often through the creation of what he calls virtual worlds, "a constructed representation of the real world of practice" (p. 157) in which the professional can, so to speak, stop the clock and explore by "reflecting on the 'back talk' from a situation, questioning the assumptional structure of knowing-in-action, and conducting on-the-spot experiments. This reflection-in-action may be a central characteristic of a creative response to surprises encountered in practice" (Mink, Rogers & Watkins, 1989, p. 11).

Schön (1987) describes the dialogue between teacher and learner in coaching situations as reflection-in-action. He notes, "Their dialogue has three essential features: it takes place in the context of the student's attempts to design; it makes use of actions as well as words; and it depends on reciprocal reflection-in-action" (p. 101). Teachers and students alternatively talk, listen, demonstrate, and imitate. Schön uses an adaptation of the ladder of inference, which he calls the ladder of reflection, to describe such learning. At times, the dialogue proceeds without a need to reflect back on values and beliefs that govern one's actions, much as in single-loop learning. But when the coach and learner get stuck—often because of different perceptions of the situation that each holds but does not share or test out with the other—they would best engage in double-loop learning to identify the hidden assumptions and beliefs that block learning. In such cases, they move up the ladder of reflection to examine the data of their interaction, come to a new understanding of what took place, decide on an alternative action, and move back down the ladder of reflection to try out this new option.

An Example. A classroom situation sheds light on the three metaphors of learning introduced at the beginning of this chapter. An instructor who believes in learning from experience and in the

brain metaphor designed a course on staff development and training around student-experienced problems relevant to the topic. In
the first class, the students developed these examples, which were
listed on a flip chart. As the students worked in small groups to
further analyze their experiences, one of the students asked the
instructor how the class could be adapted to meet her need to test
the relevance of these learning theories in cross-cultural situations.
The instructor first responded from a machine metaphor perspective, even though she had espoused a theory of learning that is more
in line with a systems perspective, that is, that the class would be
built around student-initiated concerns. Thinking on line about the
time limits of the class, but not out loud, she suggested that a block
of time could be set aside for the topic of cross-cultural learning and
that the student could do her project on this topic.

     After the class, the instructor reconstructed the situation and
pondered on the assumptions she held about learning that led to the
machine-like solution with which she was no longer comfortable.
She realized that she had acted on the following assumptions that
contradicted her espoused beliefs: that she had to be the expert who
figured out and explained the relevance of the topic of learning
theories to cross-cultural settings, that she had to control the classroom to ensure that certain topics were covered within the time
constraints, that she had to set aside a time block for a topic rather
than encourage people to collaboratively inquire into the cross-
cultural validity of various topics, and that she was responsible for
managing both the topics and the time constraints so she could not
fully design the class around the learners' experiences because she
could not unilaterally figure out how to do so within those time
constraints. She decided to use the ladder of reflection in the next
class and engage the learners in an analysis of this situation, which
clearly showed how her actions contradicted the brain metaphor
type of learning she had advocated.

     Using tools similar to those described above for action sci-
ence, she could see that her ladder of inference moved from the
actual request made by the student to the interpretation that if she
did not control the learning situation, she could not cover the material and then she might not be perceived by the students as competent. Yet, by responding in this way, she was illustrating the kind of
teacher behavior that she had just finished advocating against in a
discussion of the reasons why workplace learning was often ineffec-

tive. She could also see that the adoption of a systems perspective in learning, one that called for balancing everyone's needs, put her in a perceived double bind. If she tried to meet everyone's needs in the short time the class met, as she advocated, she did not see how she could create a coherent, unifying thread and cover what *she* thought was important for them to learn. If she abandoned someone's needs (including her own needs), however, someone would be dissatisfied and she would have created an imbalance in the system.

By constructing a virtual world with the class (in other words, a simulated laboratory in which action can be stopped and replayed in endless combinations as it can in a computer simulation), it is possible to move up and down the ladder of reflection and mutually inquire into the instructor's perceived binds and assumptions as well as to have students identify and explore their own assumptions in learning. Since the class was about staff development and training, the instructor thus would also be modelling the kind of learning that she had advocated.

Strategies to Enhance Practice. Schön (1983, 1987) is concerned with the development of professional skills and artistry in individuals, but like Argyris, he examines the individual as part of a larger system, in this case, professional schools. Schön (1987) recommends a reflective practicum in which experience becomes the starting point rather than the ending point of professional development. Instead of teaching theories and then providing an opportunity to practice them in the "real world," Schön suggests that the students be continuously involved in experiences in the real world that are then brought into the classroom for analysis. He describes three models of coaching that can be used in this reflective practicum: joint experimentation, "Follow me!," and the hall of mirrors.

In joint experimentation, "the coach's skill comes first to bear on the task of helping a student formulate the qualities she wants to achieve and then, by demonstration or description, explore different ways of producing them" (Schon, 1987, p. 296). The coach takes the lead in moving up and down the ladder of reflection and the student takes the risk of experimenting with new ways of thinking and acting. The coach walks a thin line between doing the work for the student and abdicating responsibility for sharing his or her considerable experience. Ideally, the coach generates alternatives for the student, who then makes choices and experiments with the consequences. Schön points out, however, that this kind of dialogue can only take place when the student has an idea of what he or she wants to produce. If not, or if the instructor wants to help the learner grasp an entirely different way of seeing or acting, the "Follow me!" method is better.

In "Follow me!," the coach arranges for an entire experience that incorporates times in which the coach and the student examine pieces of the on-going action of practicing one's profession by using the ladder of reflection. Here the coach takes a stronger lead in demonstrating, and the student in imitating, but the entire experience is periodically subjected to reflective dialogue. The coach must be able to present an idea from many different perspectives, and the student must be able to put aside his or her own point of view to entertain and try out these many new perspectives.

The final model, the hall of mirrors, is appropriate at a higher level of ability when the coach and the student can continually change viewpoints: "They see their interaction at one moment as a reenactment of some aspect of the student's practice; at another, as a dialogue about it; and at still another, as a modeling of its redesign" (Schon, 1987, p. 197). The interaction parallels the practice in which the students are engaged, as in the example above about the class on staff development and training, so that the students can see the connection between the virtual and actual worlds of practice. The teacher, in this case, models the kind of thinking and acting that he or she advocates be adopted by the students.

The strategies recommended by Schön in doing this coaching resemble those discussed above for action science. He suggests the following steps for unbinding a learning bind when the coach and student get stuck in their dialogue:

- Focus attention on the present interaction as an object of reflection in its own right.

- Get in touch with and describe one's own largely tacit knowing-in-action.

- Reflect on the other's understanding of the substantive material that the instructor wants to convey and the student wants to learn.

- Test what one has understood of the other's knowing-in-action and framing of the interaction; test what the other has made of one's own attempts at communication.

- Reflect on the interpersonal theories-in-use brought to the communicative process. (Schon, 1987, pp. 138–139)

Action Learning

A third approach to critically reflective learning is that of action learning. Action learning is similar to action science in that its focus is on whether or not problems are properly framed and on learning strategies that promote what Revans (1971, 1982) calls the "questioning insight" needed for dealing with new, ambiguous situations where prescriptive "programmed" learning from the past is not appropriate. During the nationalization of the coal industry, Revans discovered that he could help people learn effectively in teams working on real-life problems. Revans was a successful physicist. He and his colleagues—whom he called "comrades in adversity"—found that they learned best by regularly gathering as a team to help whoever was obviously failing at his work. In other words, failure was an opportunity for learning, not blame, through critical examination of a situation by the entire group.

Action learning as a program strategy is similar to Schön's (1987) reflective practicum; that is, actual experience is the centerpiece of learning. While action learning has been designed in many different ways (Pedler, 1983), its essence remains work on a real-life project for the purpose of learning how to learn. Unlike the previous strategies, action learning is least likely to take place in a formal classroom setting. Rather, it is a form of informal learning in which individuals might work on a project alone, but more commonly, they work with several other people. In these teams, or teams set up for this purpose if they work alone, they reflect on the way in which they frame and tackle the problem, the way in which they learn, and the way in which they interact with others in this process. The teams are facilitated by advisors who help the group design strategies for dealing with the problem, help them examine the dynamics of the group, and help them understand themselves as learners. Managers come together in informal reflective learning groups to reflect on the ongoing work they are doing in a project. Thus, they will alternate between the work setting and the learning setting with the activities in both settings forming grist for reflective learning.

When learning is at its best, people engage in both single- and double-loop learning. The strategies for critically reflective learning in this approach depend greatly on the artistry of the team advisor who functions more like a guide than a traditional classroom teacher. Unlike action science, there are no universally advocated methods that can be described, though they are key elements in the process which typically occur. Marsick (1990) identified some of the strategies used by team advisors for critically reflective learning: (1) problem framing and testing, (2) challenging norms, and (3) giving feedback.

Problem Framing and Testing. In action learning, as in action science, the team advisor or facilitator believes that learners do not often thoroughly appreciate the nature of the complex, systemic problems they are facing before they begin jumping to solutions. One reason for this is that although a rational analysis of alternatives is emphasized in problem solving, solutions seldom produce the results that were intended for reasons that are not rational and are more likely to be emotional or attitudinal. Thus, one strategy for critically reflective learning is to help learners adequately frame problems. Problem framing involves seeing the situation from many different perspectives, which often takes time and involves a series of experiments to test alternative hypotheses about the nature of the situation.

However, managers, like other learners, frequently want to jump immediately to solutions. One manager, who worked on a project in which a fertilizer company was looking into exports, described the key role of the project advisor at this early stage. The project advisor "guided us on our tour to concentrate on the problems, to define the problems. . . . Immediately when there is some kind of solution coming up, everyone was discussing the solution. So, back to square one. . . . he would say, 'wait a minute, where are you? what are you doing?' "

Questions, especially those that may seem "silly," are central to bringing different perspectives to bear on a problem. One staff member, for example, saw his key role as "very much to put the question in another way." One manager described the way in which questions linked the creation of multiple perspectives with problem reformulation. "In the beginning, you have a kind of situation where (they have to) learn that they can think about the problem in different ways. They are very often quick to say this is the problem. . . . they very seldom try to challenge their problem definitions." Then the advisor can ask silly or challenging questions and help the group think through how to test their perceptions.

Another strategy to enlarge one's framing of the problem is drawing out and contraposing differences: "You don't reflect on things until you . . . have some sort of contrast . . . between both sides, between managers and the host company, or it could be between different areas of belief within the host company, it could even be between me and them, or whatever." Project advisors also design activities on the spot whereby a situation could be looked at from different points of view. One advisor, for example, talked about a discussion with three members of his project group and some top executives of the insurance company with which they were working. The executives were about to leave but the group had made no progress, so "I asked them not to leave but just sit for a half hour and listen to the group." He asked the group to reflect on the conversation thus far while the executives listened to them, in a kind of fish bowl (in which a small group forms a circle in the center of a larger group which sits in an outer circle to observe the inner group's process) where they could not interrupt until the advisor let them. After a half hour, he opened discussion up to everyone and found that both the project team and the executives could see things very differently than they had before.

Norm Challenging. As participants engage in learning, they often come up against perceived norms and expectations that they begin to challenge with the help of the instructor. Questioning and drawing out contrasts, described above as strategies to open up alternative viewpoints, can also help get learners to challenge their norms about learning and the teaching/learning transaction. So too can the collaborative way in which the program is designed. For example, one participant described the way in which his program group took over the teaching design on the second day of his program and replaced one of the speakers on time management whom they felt was ineffective. Likewise, a group he later helped advise were subjected to "heavy" lecture-presentations to which they politely listened. The next morning the advisors surprised them by challenging their norms about proper classroom decorum by asking if they were "going to sit here 40 days and 10 months without understanding anything and (yet not) react?"

Norm challenging is most evident in the projects themselves. For example, one advisor worked with a group of managers whose fathers and grandfathers had all worked with the same company. It was particularly difficult to get the group to see the problem from different perspectives since they had so long thought in terms of one way of doing things, so the advisor suggested they take a trip up North so they could teach him about their jobs. In the course of informal conversation, they began to talk about the assumptions they held about the work and about one another. The advisor helped them reframe the problem they were working on, and then the group decided to challenge hierarchical norms in the company and invite the new chief executive officer on a similar trip to power sites to learn more about the situation.

Afterwards, the advisor realized that they had not fully comprehended the importance of what they did. He challenged them to explain their actions, asking dramatically if they had previously thought the head of the company would "bite them. . . . And I don't think it was actually only symbolic, but it was also meant, in a way, quite literally. 'Bite!' " he said, voice rising. He continued to raise questions: " 'what could have happened? (Would he bite) like a bear or wolf up in the woods where you work? Were you scared of the bears there? . . . Are you scared of him?' " The advisor asked questions and used metaphors to help "in making a picture for them, a map about this authority thing" to draw out the lessons from the experience.

Giving Feedback. A key role in learning is taking advantage of things that happen to better understand oneself as a learner. The situations faced by the managers in the action learning study frequently mirror the kinds of interactions that the learner is faced with outside the classroom, as in Schön's hall of mirrors coaching strategy discussed above. A critical ingredient for this understanding is the feedback received by the advisor and by peers. Seminars can be designed to facilitate this sharing of feedback, such as a popular weeklong activity in the action learning program studied oriented to self-discovery. Much of this was also done in the normal course of project work.

In projects, thinking and acting were subjected to feedback from the group. One manager described the way in which feedback from others enabled him to see certain aspects of himself differently. His background in negotiation made it difficult to get feedback from others "because people can't really distinguish between the person and the function." It was not clear when actions were related to his personality or wishes and when they were orders from management. Even though this manager no longer works with negotiation, "the program did suggest that this line of work has changed me in more ways than I was aware of," both in terms of positive attributes and behavior he might want to change, particularly the impression he gave others of speaking for management when he intended to speak for himself.

It was also not unusual for staff members to use group dynamics instruments at various points to help members observe the way they work and give feedback to one another. Through the dynamics of the project groups, tensions surfaced which, if brought to awareness and challenged, led to significant personal change since project experiences were often typical of other work experiences.

In summary, action learning provides another approach for critically reflective learning. There is no one way to facilitate action learning, but some of the strategies used in one illustrative program included the following: problem framing, which involved getting people to see things from multiple perspectives, formulating and testing alternative hypotheses about the situation; norm challenging; and giving feedback.

SKILLS NEEDED TO FACILITATE CRITICALLY REFLECTIVE LEARNING

In this final section, skills needed to facilitate critically reflective learning in light of the above strategies and the three metaphors of learning will be examined: the machine, the system, and the brain. It is tempting to develop a list of do's and don'ts; but, to return to the starting point of this chapter, any technique or method can be used differently depending on a teacher's point of view. So instead, the roles of the teacher vis-à-vis critically reflective learning will be explored.

A framework developed by Watkins (1989) of alternative roles for human resource developers will be adapted here to explore the role of the facilitator of learning in classroom settings. The roles were those of the developer of human capital, problem solver, the change agent/interventionist, the designer, and the empowerer. While, at least on the surface, each role may seem more relevant to learning as described by one of the above metaphors, we also look at ways in which some roles incorporate thinking from several metaphorical perspectives.

Developer of Human Capital

The teacher as a developer of human capital is, on the surface, a role which seems most compatible with the machine metaphor where learners are expected to master predefined knowledge and skills to better accommodate themselves to needs set by others more powerful in society. Human capital theory points out that the learners' value or capital is enhanced when they increase their learning in areas that are in demand in the marketplace. The teacher's role is to help learners acquire desired skills and achieve goals which are set by society. Critics of human capital theories point out the role of education as a means of social control, reinforcement of the inherent class structure, and the objectification of people. On the other hand, individuals gain considerably more from education than simply an enhanced economic value. Intrinsic satisfaction, enhanced life skills, increased capacity to function effectively as a parent and a citizen—all are alternative benefits derived from learning.

Critically reflective learning may seem incompatible with this role, at first glance. However, even if the teacher and learners do subscribe to this point of view, they can become more aware of the way in which social forces mold their choices. They can also use some of the above strategies for learning, such as skills in reflection-in-action, to increase their competence within existing social structures. Finally, individuals have greatest "value" to themselves and to society when they have an enhanced capacity to learn continuously.

Problem Solver

Much popular adult learning theory looks at the role teachers can play in helping learners solve problems. The problem-solving role is enacted through the use of systems theory because all systems are made up of the same parts—context, inputs, processes, outputs, and feedback. These parts not only help clarify the elements of a system, but have definable characteristics which can be tinkered with to produce alternative outputs. However, this perspective can lead the trainer to solve the wrong problem because of inadequate mental models. The systems approach, when conceptualized broadly, may be a useful model for addressing the problems of short term perspectives, truncated problem-solving processes, or limited world views.

Change Agent/Interventionist

Change theory traces its roots to Kurt Lewin's (1938, 1948) work on life space, the social field, and group dynamics, which has also been directly influential in the work of Argyris and Schön and is at least indirectly influential in many action learning programs because of the necessary concern with group dynamics. Change theorists often subscribe to a systems perspective since they are aware of the impact that each person in a group or organization has on others within and outside the group. Action science and action learning, for example, involve systems perspectives, but go beyond the descriptive perspective of systems theory to a more normative or prescriptive model which describes what should be rather than what is.

The role of the interventionist also goes beyond such passive roles as that of the humanistic facilitator who makes sure everyone has an equal opportunity to participate. The interventionist has a point of view about the situation which is not imposed upon the group, but which may be publicly advocated and tested, and is certainly used to guide group members into situations and activities that will help them develop a point of view. The interventionist is not afraid to feed back to individuals or groups what he or she sees occurring directly and by illustrating assertions with data. The interventionist actively assists the groups in seeing the situation from many points of view and in formulating and testing their own hypotheses. In short, the person in this role has the clear objective of *intervening* or bringing about change in the learner.

Designer

Design theory is also based on a systems perspective. In organizations, design involves diagnosing and selecting the structure and formal system of communication, authority, and responsibility to achieve organizational goals. Design can be examined at the level of individuals, as Schön (1983, 1987) does when looking at the way in which professionals, students, and coaches design their responses to a puzzling situation. Or, it can be at the level of whole organizations. In the teaching and learning transaction, design is evident in the way in which teachers and learners construct their moments of interaction.

Simon (1965) distinguishes between programmed activity,

prompted by a single clear stimulus, to which the learned response can be fairly routine; and unprogrammed activity which calls for the design of wholly new responses. In the latter, professionals draw on their past knowledge and experience in applying rules to a new situation. If the stimulus clearly calls for application of a known rule, then decision making is routine and little new learning is called for. Unprogrammed activity is exactly the opposite. An unprogrammed activity is evoked when there is no tried and true method for handling the stimulus either because it is a new situation, its nature is elusive and complex, or because it is so important that it deserves a customized response. Unprogrammed activity has three stages of individual activity:

1. *Intelligence activity,* or searching the environment for conditions calling for a decision

2. *Design activity*—inventing, developing, and analyzing courses of action

3. *Choice activity*—selecting a course of action from those available

Design can be looked at prescriptively and rather linearly, as in the machine metaphor, or interactively, involving many stakeholders, as in the systems metaphor. In addition, the brain metaphor adds the dimension of continual experimentation by people engaged in collaborative inquiry. The teacher helps learners to be sensitive to puzzles and surprises that might signal an opportunity for learning, to bring multiple perspectives to bear upon a situation, to challenge expectations and beliefs, and to hold "reflective conversations with the situation." In doing this, the teacher is designing a process through which unprogrammed activity in the learning situation can be routinely programmed.

Empowerer

This role is oriented to transformation and emancipation and has its roots in critical theory, which Geuss (1981) summarized. According to Geuss, emancipation is defined as the movement, or transformation, from an initial state to a final state in which (1) the initial state is one of false consciousness, error, and unfree existence; (a) this false consciousness is interconnected with the oppression; (b) this oppression is self-imposed and the false consciousness is self-designed; (c) the power in the above lies in the fact that individuals do not realize that their oppression is self-imposed; (2) in the final state, individuals are free of false consciousness, enlightened, and free of self-imposed constraints (emancipated). Examples of critical theory include psychoanalysis, aimed at individuals; Marxism, aimed at social systems; and action science, aimed at organizations.

Empowerment is compatible with the brain metaphor in that it aims, in part, at dialogue among members of a group who are equals and have access to full and complete information.

Teachers may not feel comfortable, however, with a role that touches on what they perceive to be therapy or a political critique of the system in which they or their learners work and live. Action science is well-suited to a learning perspective that can be empowering, especially when the emotions involved in these changes are acknowledged and worked through.

Empowerment carries political overtones, even though the teacher may not subscribe to a Marxist perspective on change or may not intend to change the system in which teacher and learners live and work. However, as many educators acknowledge, learning is not a neutral, value-free process. There is a risk in enabling people to identify and examine the assumptions on which their actions are based since these assumptions are often influenced by larger political, social, and cultural values that the learner may wish to take action to change. Empowerment suggests an emancipation from something and an enhancement of one's personal power. Embedded in each of these suggestions is an implicit statement of value—that emancipation is needed and that increased personal power is desirable. These assumptions have clear political implications. Thus, the teacher as empowerer may encourage learners to challenge the power relationships in the classroom, including the teacher's formal power as well the learners' willingness to have power over their own learning.

CONCLUSION

This chapter offers new paradigms for critically reflective learning. See Figure 4.2 for a summary. New approaches to the learning and teaching transactional process are needed which inte-

LEARNING METAPHORS	TEACHING STRATEGIES	TEACHING ROLES
Machine		Developer of Human Capital
System		Problem Solver Change Agent/ Interventionist Designer
Brain	Action Science *Language Analysis* *Surfacing Thoughts* *Ladder of Inference*	Empowerer
	Reflection-in-Action *Joint* *Experimentation* *Follow Me!* *The Hall of Mirrors*	
	Action Learning *Problem Framing* *& Testing* *Challenging Norms* *Giving Feedback*	

Figure 4.2 *Summary of new paradigms for teaching and learning.*

grate more holistic metaphors of the process. Methods which successfully call on learners to learn and simultaneously reflect on how and why they are learning as they are have much greater potential for preparing adults to function successfully in this complex era of information. Metaphors which describe the nature of the learning process include the machine, the system, and the brain. Strategies which facilitate critically reflective learning and which are consistent with the brain metaphor which is advocated here include action science, action learning, and reflection-in-action. Metaphors are also used to depict the role of the teacher. These include the teacher as developer of human capital, problem-solver, change agent or interventionist, designer, and empowerer. Each of these teaching roles can be enacted from any one of the three metaphors or perspectives on learning. Effective facilitators of adult learning in the information age will be familiar with each of these paradigms and able to adopt a variety of teaching roles. At the level of expert professional practice, these facilitators will be able to use strategies which call on learners to reflect critically.

REFERENCES

Argyris, C., & Schön, D. A. (1974). *Theory in practice: Increasing professional effectiveness.* San Francisco: Jossey-Bass.

Argyris, C., & Schön, D. A. (1978). *Organizational learning: A theory of action perspective.* San Francisco: Jossey-Bass.

Argyris, C., Putnam, R., & Smith, D. M. (1985). *Action science.* San Francisco: Jossey-Bass.

Ashby, W. R. (1952). *Design for a brain.* New York: John Wiley.

Brookfield, S. D. (1987). *Developing critical thinkers: Challenging adults to explore alternative ways of thinking and acting.* San Francisco: Jossey-Bass.

Geuss, R. (1981). *The idea of a critical theory.* New York: Cambridge University Press.

Lewin, K. (1938). *The conceptual representation of the measurement of psychological forces.* Durham: Duke University Press.

Lewin, K. (1948). *Resolving social conflicts.* New York: Harper & Row.

Lincoln, Y. S. (1985). *Organizational theory and inquiry: The paradigm revolution.* Beverly Hills: Sage.

Marsick, V. J. (Ed.). (1987). *Learning in the workplace.* London: Croom Helm.

Marsick, V. J. (1990). Action learning in the workplace. In J. Mezirow & Associates, *Fostering critical self-reflection in adulthood* (pp. 23–46). San Francisco: Jossey-Bass.

Marsick, V. J., & Watkins, K. E. (1990). *Informal and incidental learning: A challenge to HRD.* London: Routledge.

Mink, O., Rogers, R., & Watkins, K. (1989). Creative leadership: Discovering paradoxes of innovation and risk. *Contemporary Educational Psychology, 14,* 1–13.

Mitroff, I. (1983). *Stakeholders of the organizational mind.* San Francisco: Jossey-Bass.

Morgan, G. (1986). *Images of organization.* Beverly Hills: Sage.

Pedler, M. (Ed.) (1983). *Action learning in practice,* Aldershot, Hants, U. K.: Gower.

Revans, R.W. (1971). *Developing effective managers: A new approach to business education.* New York: Praeger & London: Longmans.

Revans, R. W. (1982). *The origin and growth of action learning.* Bickely, Kent: Chartwell-Bratt & Lund, Sweden: Studenlitteratur.

Schön, D. A. (1983). *The reflective practitioner.* New York: Basic Books.

Schön, D. A. (1987). *Educating the reflective practitioner.* San Francisco: Jossey-Bass.

Simon, H.A. (1965). Administrative decision making, *Public Administration Review, 25,* 31–37.

Watkins, K. E. (1989). Five metaphors: Alternative theories for human resource development. In D. Gradous & R. Swanson (Eds.), *Systems theory applied to human resource development* (pp. 167–184). Alexandria: University of Minnesota Training & Development Research Center and ASTD Press.

Weick, K. (1983). Managerial thought in the context of action. In S. Srivastava and Associates (Eds.), *The executive mind: New insights on managerial thought and action* (pp. 221–242). San Francisco: Jossey-Bass.

CHAPTER 5

Adult Learning Methods and Techniques

MICHAEL W. GALBRAITH
BONNIE S. ZELENAK

Numerous methods and techniques can be used to enhance an educational encounter (Galbraith, 1990). However, not all methods will complement the adult learning transactional process and adhere to the essential characteristics of collaboration, challenge, critical reflection, and praxis. This chapter will examine seven adult learning methods and techniques that seem most appropriate for the transactional process: discussion, simulation, learning contracts, inquiry teams, case method, critical incident, and mentoring. Approaches that utilize technology to enhance the teaching and learning transaction will be discussed in Chapter 6 by Blackwood and White.

DISCUSSION

Discussion is perhaps the most widely preferred method. If properly implemented, it should result in a collaborative, challenging, reflective, transforming, and democratic process. The discussion method has been recognized as the adult education method par excellence (Lindeman, 1926; Bergevin, Morris, & Smith, 1963; Paterson, 1970; Houle, 1972; Brookfield, 1985, 1986, 1990; Knox, 1986). Such status results from its benefits of participatory learning, equality among facilitators and learners, and democratic associations. Brookfield (1985) suggests that definitions of discussion "seem to cluster at different points along a continuum distinguished by the degree of control that the teacher exercises over discussion procedures and content" (p. 56). At one end of the continuum is controlled discussion whereby the teacher has strict control over the direction as well as the amount of comments and questions that will be solicited from the learners. At the other end the discussion is open and free-flowing and welcomes teachable movements that result from unanticipated learning events. It is from this perspective that the discussion method will be examined.

What is the purpose of discussion? Primarily it is oriented toward a cognitive change and the quality of purposeful conversation and deliberation (Bergevin, Morris, & Smith, 1963). It is not directed at the notion that all members within the discussion group make equal length verbal contributions. Brookfield (1990) writes that the most impelling cognitive purposes for discussion use should be:

• To expose learners to a diversity of perspectives on an issue, topic, or theme;

• To help learners to externalize the assumptions underlying their values, beliefs, and actions;

• To assist learners in perspective taking; that is, in coming to see the world as others see it;

• To introduce learners to elements of complexity and ambiguity in an issue, topic, or theme. (p. 192)

All this should help learners become critical thinkers who question and scrutinize their held assumptions, beliefs, values, and actions, while at the same time helping them to become more reflective and aware of their contextuality (Brookfield, 1987). Discussion can provide, in a nonthreatening and nonjudgmental manner, a setting for exploration and debate of contrasting positions. Such risk-taking and challenging educational encounters can occur in a supportive fashion that allows learners to lose their apprehension and explore uncharted courses of learning.

The discussion method is found in formal and nonformal educational settings. Special interest groups such as AIDS support groups, single parents, family members of terminally ill relatives, substance abusers, feminists, homosexuals, and others have typically used a collaborative discussion method to help them "seek a reinforcement of their self-worth" and "to create new meaning systems" (Brookfield, 1986, p. 142). Within nonformal settings leadership for the discussion, as well as the process of interpreting or analyzing what has been voiced, may be constantly shifting from one individual to another. In more formal educational encounters, such as college level seminars or courses, the facilitator may be responsible for the preparation of the discussion session. Essential elements in that preparation will briefly be detailed.

Preparing for Discussion

One of the first responsibilities is the selection of discussion themes, issues, topics, and questions that form the focus of the discussion. Brookfield (1986) states that the questions to be discussed "should not be too factual or too uncontroversial, and they should not be answerable in the course of preparatory reading by the group" (p. 140). Discussion should be guided by controversial issues that can be viewed as having various opinions and possible interpretations. Second, learners should have access before the scheduled session to the materials that will be under scrutiny. Effective planning enhances the likelihood that learners will have read the pertinent materials and will have a common set of ideas, concepts, and factual information to guide the topic under discussion. Another essential condition that must be met, if a productive discussion is to occur, is for members of the group to devise what rules or moral codes of conduct will guide the session (Brookfield, 1990). If a clear code of conduct can be established, Brookfield suggests that minority opinions, as well as silent group members, will be respected, no one individual will dominate the group discussion, divergent viewpoints will be tolerated, and if desired the confidentiality of opinions expressed can be ensured.

Other essential components that need attention in the preparation process are the group size and the learners' backgrounds and experiences. Knox (1986) suggests that a discussion group should be composed of between ten and twenty participants. The appropriate number is essential if a meaningful and provocative discussion is to occur. It is also important to try to acquire information about the participants' backgrounds and experiences. A heterogeneous group will have many viewpoints. Such a diverse group can hopefully encourage others involved in the discussion to experience alternative ways of thinking about their assumptions, values, beliefs, and actions. It allows learners to address an issue from a different perspective than the one they usually embrace. Finally, if this diversity is considered, then the necessity to personalize the discussion topics so learners can make connections between their experiences and some broader themes seems apparent (Brookfield, 1990). Facilitators can ask learners to think in personalized ways and to encourage the exploration within the discussion session of what relevance these newfound discoveries have for their personal, political, or professional lives. Personalizing the discussion topics can add a new dimension and significance to the learning encounter.

The Discussion Session

If one word categorizes discussion it has to be unpredictability. Brookfield states "If we knew exactly what was going to happen in a session it would cease to be a discussion in any meaningful sense" (1990, p. 195). The approach that you use in facilitating a discussion may not be useful or effective in all discussion sessions. A prescriptive approach to discussion leadership is nonexistent. Understanding the immediate specific situation and what you feel will work effectively is based many times on your insights and intuitions or what Schön (1983) calls a theory-in-use. Because every session will most likely be different (even when you have the same group of learners), it is important to have a reservoir of discussion leads, materials, and possible questions (Brookfield, 1990). Flexibility is a key factor in a discussion session if it is to be open, free-flowing, and democratic. Some of the most exciting and meaningful learning moments are those that are unplanned and unanticipated. Facilitators and learners must be willing to welcome the unanticipated and to see these happenings as very teachable moments and an opportunity to explore new dimensions that can hold new significance and meaning.

Incorporated into any discussion are the undercurrents of caring, listening, and strong feelings. Understanding and attending to the emotional dimensions that take place within a discussion are essential (Brookfield, 1990; Daloz, 1986). Controversial topics generate emotionally packed responses and feelings. It is important not to downplay the emotional temper of the group but to utilize and encourage that dimension. It can serve as a way of connecting what is meaningful and important to the learners. Facilitators need to value and understand the fundamental role it plays in the interpretation and renegotiation of learners' assumptions and actions. In Chapter 2 Brookfield suggests using learning journals as a way of keeping informed of the emotional dimensions of the group's discussions.

With all the diversity and emotional dimensions associated with an open discussion method, how do you know if the discussion was effective and meaningful? If the discussion has been highly controversial and emotional, participants including the facilitator may leave feeling disturbed and uneasy because it has thrown their beliefs, values, and actions into doubt and at the present time they are unable to make the connection or understand the relevance to their lives. Such a scenario may be evaluated as more successful than one that leaves the learners feeling comfortable but unchallenged. As Brookfield (1990) writes "A discussion which learners leave feeling comfortable may well be one in which their prejudices are confirmed and their habitual patterns of reasoning are reinforced . . . such sessions may be pleasant social occasions, but they are hardly educational" (p. 200). From this it can be suggested that discussion cannot be evaluated strictly by learner satisfaction. Discussions that are characterized by pain, fear, excitement, anger, frustration, confusion, challenge, and self-scrutiny may be the most educationally productive sessions because such discussions encourage participants to call into question their habitual givens. Educational activities can be considered successful when participants reach out for closure to questions; when they begin to realize the connection between what is being discussed and the relationship it has to their lives. Discussion can be evaluated as successful when learners have been helped by the activity to think critically and reflectively, although at times this may be painful and disturbing.

SIMULATION

Simulation is the imitation or representation of one system by a device or technique that replicates the dynamics of the first system. Simulations are useful complements to theoretical learning and are beneficial when used to test out theories, ideologies, and hypotheses. By design, simulations provide opportunities for more direct experience with a particular phenomenon than do lectures and seminars. A simulation entails setting up situations that approximate reality and then having learners act out the situations. It is most beneficial to learning when followed by discussion and evaluation.

Enhancement of Learning and Action

Simulations enable learners to actively engage in experiential educational encounters that provide for reflective thinking and alternative ways of incorporating this new reflectivity into action. Kolb (1981) suggests that developing an understanding of the learning process promises a dual reward "a more refined epistemology that defines the varieties of truth and interrelationships and a greater psychological understanding of how individuals acquire knowledge in its different forms" (p. 234). In his experiential learning theory Kolb maintains that learning is conceived as a four-stage cycle with (1) concrete experience serving as the basis for (2) observations and reflections which are used in (3) the formation of abstract concepts and generalizations (or theory building) from which the individual (4) tests implications of concepts in new situations. These implications guide the individual in the creation of new experiences. Kolb's model suggests that learning requires abilities that are at polar extremes and that there are two primary dimensions to the learning process. The first represents concrete experience at one end and abstract conceptualization at the other. The second dimension represents active experimentation at one extreme and reflective observation at the other. Kolb (1981) concludes that "in the process of learning, one moves in varying degrees from actor to observer, from specific involvement to general analytic detachment" (p. 236). The extremes of functioning on these dimensions represent opposing definitions of competence and functioning. That is, reflection tends to inhibit action and vice versa; abstract reasoning leads to detachment of ego from the outer world or from inner experience and to the enhancement of reflectivity while concreteness represents the absence of these abilities.

How can simulations enhance learning and reasoning or reflection and action, especially if reflection inhibits action and if concrete experiences are at a polar extreme to abstract reasoning? Kolb (1981) provides some insight when he suggests that a learner needs to proceed along the learning continuum and must experience all phases of the process if learning is to be meaningful. Every dimension in Kolb's model is important in the learning process in that each is needed for the enhancement of the others. As learners move from actors to observers they reflect upon immediate experiences at hand and have a deeper understanding of those experiences. Simulations, by design, incorporate the actor/observer functions within the exercises. For example, in a well-designed role-playing exercise (one example of a simulation) the actors' and observers' roles and feelings are well defined. During the debriefing session, a necessary ingredient in simulation exercises, actors and observers exchange perspectives and interpretations on the events that transpired in the role play. Through dialogue a more in-depth understanding of assumptions and behaviors can be created. Furthermore, actors and observers are provided the opportunity to exchange positions so that each may experience the position of the former.

Benefits

Some of the benefits of simulations include enhanced motivation among participants as they physically act out specific scenarios and reason their way through the probable consequences of behavior. Brookfield (1987) states that crisis-decision simulations, in which people make difficult choices from among several uncomfortable options, require people to justify their reasons for selecting one option over another. When justifying their rationale for choosing a particular course of action "their assumptions (in particular, their basic moral values) will be at least partially revealed" (p. 107). It is through this self-reflection that change occurs. Daloz (1986) states that "it is only by bringing our changes into conscious awareness that we can be assured that they will stay put" (p. 213).

Simulations liven up what might otherwise become deadly routines. They can be as short as a two minute role play to enhance awareness of a given principle, or as long as a semester game to focus on complex decision-making and problem-solving skills. Simulation exercises help participants understand the thinking of those whose place they play in the given situation. They help people identify, investigate, and challenge long held assumptions that influence their thoughts and actions.

Role of the Facilitator

It should be noted that, despite the benefits to be accrued, investigating assumptions is difficult. Skilled facilitators must pre-

pare the participants for the exercise, provide clear and understandable instructions, determine whether the purpose of the exercise is
understood by all learners, and be able to judge the amount of
ambiguity and cognitive dissonance that people can tolerate. They
must also have a sense of the group dynamics and be skillful at
developing strategies that will encourage all members to fully participate in the process. Under these circumstances it may be beneficial to use nonthreatening examples when designing the simulation.
Participants who find the exercise too personally unsettling and
disturbing may choose to remove themselves from the group rather
than continue the simulation. Facilitators must be sensitive to these
possibilities and must plan the simulation in a way that will benefit
the group to best advantage.

Many kinds of simulations can be developed to enhance
adult learning. Examples include computer simulations, educational games, role reversal, in-basket exercises, and role play. Role
play is one of the most commonly used simulation exercises that
depict the essential elements of the transactional process.

Role Playing

Role playing is the spontaneous acting out of an incident by
several members of a group. Its purpose is to convey human relationships and interactions and how these factors influence the outcome
of a situation. Through role playing, participants explore and, under the best of circumstances, develop an understanding of the perceptions and emotions of others, thus gaining greater insight into
the complexity of human relationships, issues, and problems. Several procedures are usually incorporated into the role-playing design. A problem or issue is typically presented to a group of individuals who are asked to perform designated roles. Behaviors are impro-
vised to fit with the assigned roles. The benefits of role playing
include: giving participants practice in applying principles learned,
developing insights into human relations, providing concrete examples of theoretical concepts, maintaining interest, and providing a
nonthreatening channel to express feelings (Bernstein, 1976). A major value to participants is that it helps them "integrate the cognitive
and affective dimensions of their learning" (Brookfield, 1987, p.
104).

Roles of Participants and Observers. It is important that role-
playing exercises be carefully structured. Facilitators need to have a

clear purpose or objective for the simulation; participants need clear descriptions of the roles they are to play including the attitudes of the players, as well as an understanding of how the setting is defined. A role-playing situation typically involves from two to five players. The remainder of the group should observe the simulation, making note of patterns of interaction, such as who initiates topics, recommends actions to be taken, or disregards other's opinions. Observers play an important role in the discussion that follows and should disclose their observations to the actors. Each group's understanding of the other's motivations will be enhanced through such dialogue.

In role-playing exercises participants should be given the opportunity to volunteer for roles. Minimal time is needed for the players to develop their parts, and the facilitator must be cautious about leaving too much time for each activity. Once the main points of the role play are made, discussion should follow. Players should be given an opportunity to discuss the situation with the rest of the group. The class should then discuss their reactions to the simulation including responses to trenchant or accommodating behaviors, strategies used by players that brought about desired results, background information that inhibited progress on the situation presented, and possible strategies that the players might have used to develop alternative reactions. At this point it is possible for the facilitator to ask to replay, to alter a situation within the simulation, or to conclude the role play.

Benefits. The benefits of role playing include showing the strengths, weaknesses, and consequences of certain behaviors or attitudes; depicting divergent points of view; exploring interpersonal relations; and bringing to life theoretical or philosophical concepts. Other benefits include bringing novelty into the adult learning situation, providing for active participation by group members, bringing real life job or education-related problems of group members (who volunteer them) into the classroom, providing several solutions to a problem, and arousing interest (Bernstein, 1976; Morgan, Holmes, & Bundy, 1976).

According to Brookfield (1987), "In terms of helping people identify and analyze their taken-for-granted assumptions, the variant of role play known commonly as role reversal is probably the most effective technique" (p. 106). This technique is often used in negotiations seminars, marital counseling, and industrial relations training. Through role reversal the actors assume the roles with which they come in frequent contact but which they do not experience themselves. During the discussion session participants reflect upon the roles that they played as well as on the behaviors of their partners. Since one of the partners played the role of the first person, the first person has the rare opportunity of witnessing how others see him or her, how others act or what they say while filling the position of the first person. Participants can observe and analyze the behaviors and words of the person playing their real life role and come to a deeper self-understanding.

Limitations. There are potential limitations of role playing. By its very nature it can take on very personal overtones. The facilitator must know how to guide the activity, where to set limits, and when to let the imagination of participants soar. The group can go on tangents that are unrelated or even deleterious to the purpose of the exercise if proper limits are not established. The follow-up discussion is important to understanding the meaning of whatever transpired. Without a proper review the exercise may appear to be unfocused or, worse yet, unimportant to the stated purpose. Role playing may not always be an appropriate method, particularly if there is only one answer to a problem. It takes time and can be overused. It can be ineffective if the role players are unfamiliar with the problems associated with the simulation, and it can lead to the embarrassment of some members of the group. There is also the danger that actors will become too enamored with their acting ability and forget the purpose of the exercise. The facilitator must take these matters into consideration when setting the scene for the role play and the discussion activities that follow.

LEARNING CONTRACTS

The person most responsible for introducing the learning contract process into adult education is Malcolm Knowles (1975, 1984, 1986). He suggests that learning contracts are an alternative mechanism for structuring learning experiences for adult learners. A learning contract is a written formal agreement constructed by the learner which details the knowledge, skills, attitudes, and values that will be acquired, how the learning will be accomplished, the target date for the completion of the learning, demonstrated evidence of accomplished learning, and what specific criteria that will be used for the evaluation of the learning (Knowles, 1986; O'Donnell & Caffarella, 1990).

Learning contracts have been used most often in institutions of higher education. However, as Knowles (1986) reports, learning contracts have been incorporated into a variety of other settings as well such as business and industry human resource development departments, health agencies, governmental agencies, and religious organizations. They have been used in independent study courses, external degree programs, clinical placement activities, management development programs, staff development training, and internship development planning. Contract learning replaces a content plan with a process plan. The learner is ultimately responsible for the establishment of the plan as well as the setting of the parameters for the learning. Because the learning contract process is grounded in the belief that adult learners are diverse, this method takes into account the differences in learning styles, personal and social backgrounds, and paces of learning. It encourages adult learners to seek a higher degree of independence and self-direction in their learning encounters.

The Contract

O'Donnell and Caffarella (1990) suggest two approaches to the construction of a learning contract. In the first approach the contract may be constructed and planned entirely by the learner. In this case, no specific learning objectives have been suggested by the facilitator and thus the learner is free to pursue a learning activity in any manner desired. The second approach is where the learner constructs most or part of the contract and the planning of the learning is around established objectives that have been determined by the facilitator or the sponsoring organization. O'Donnell and Caffarella (1990) write concerning this approach that "the what to be learned may not be negotiable; however, how the learner achieves that what is open to individual discretion" (p. 135).

Writing a learning contract for the first time may be a frustrating and anxious experience for the adult learner. This is why a thoughtful explanation of contract learning is essential before the journey into the process begins. Within the discussion the theoretical and philosophical foundations of contract learning should be present (Knowles, 1986). The focus of the discussion should be around the characteristics and development of adults as learners, the concepts of independence and self-direction, learning styles, motivation, and elements of risk taking and challenge. It should encompass the changing role of the learner "from that of more or less passive receiver of transmitted information and submissive executor of the instructor's directives to that of initiative-taking planner and executor of strategies and resources for achieving mutually agreed-on objectives" (p. 44). The changing role of the facilitator from didactic transmitter of content to that of consultant, collaborator, resource person, and guide should also be discussed.

The first requirement of any learning encounter is to identify what learning needs exist. Chapter 1 explained some of the techniques for identifying and assessing learning needs (the gap between where you are now and where you want to be). The learner will be ready to begin writing the contract after this is accomplished, at least on a tentative basis. A typical learning contract is comprised of five sections: learning objectives, learning resources and strategies, target date for completion, evidence of accomplishment, and evaluation of the learning (see Figure 5.1). Each section of the contract will be described briefly.

Learning Objectives. The first column of the contract describes what the learner is going to learn. It is used to translate the identified learning needs into learning objectives. These objectives are written to describe "what you will learn, not what you will do to learn them" (Knowles, 1986, p. 29). Learners should write a specific learning objective for each identified learning need. Depending on the type of learning objective, appropriate terminology should be used that is meaningful and descriptive. Examples of learning objectives may be "To acquire knowledge about the history of adult education." "To develop the ability to describe the theoretical disjunctions between program planning models," "To increase my skill and understanding in using methods and techniques appropriate for facilitating adult learning," "To gain a knowledge of training and development settings within business and industry," and "To understand and implement the essential elements of critical reflection into my own thinking and behavior activities." Learning objectives may be written to acquire skill, knowledge, understanding, and so on. The learning objectives detailed in column one will provide the focus for the remaining sections of the learning contract.

Learning Contract

Learner _____

_____ Learning Experience _____

Learning Objectives (What are you going to learn?)	Learning Resources and Strategies (How are you going to learn it?)	Target Date	Evidence of Accomplishment (How are you going to demonstrate that you have learned it?)	Evaluation of the Learning (What are the criteria on which you will judge that your learning efforts have been successful and who will be involved in the judging process?)

Figure 5.1 Learning contract form.

Resources and Strategies. Column two is used to describe how each proposed learning objective will be accomplished. Human and material resources should be considered as learners identify the most appropriate plan for reaching the selected objectives. Resources, for example, can be books, journal articles, handouts, newspapers, a list of suggested readings, resource persons, peers, the instructor, media outlets, and so on. The strategies are the ways the identified resources will be used (Knowles, 1986). Examples of strategies may be going to the library, reading book chapters or articles identified on the assignment sheet, interviewing experts, talking with the instructor, taking a field trip, conducting an interview, making observations, completing a CD-ROM search of the literature, working in an inquiry term, and so forth. Many resources and strategies may be listed for each identified learning objective. It is important to use the most appropriate resources and strategies in addressing the learning objective. This is where the facilitator or some other resource expert can be of greatest assistance. Tapping into the expertise and knowledge base of human resources early in the process can provide some guidance and direction toward reaching the objectives as well as reducing some of the frustration and anxiety associated with developing a meaningful learning contract.

Target Date. In this column the learner puts in the date that each learning objective will be completed. Some learners like to establish a target date that they can work toward. It gives them a guide to their planning and some idea of how to manage their time more effectively in relationship to the other responsibilities in their lives.

Evidence. Column four describes the evidence that learners will collect and the activities that they may construct to achieve the stated learning objectives. The kind of evidence presented will depend on the type of objective stated. Evidence may range from writing a scholarly paper, to submitting detailed outlines from suggested readings, to creating a role play, to writing annotated bibliographies, to developing video tapes of interviews conducted, to giving an oral presentation, to writing a learning journal from the field notes taken from an observation participation experience, to the creation of some project. The possibilities of the kinds of evidence that can be generated are limitless. Within column four, the learner can also provide a detailed description of how the evidence will be organized, what will be its components, and other information that makes the evidence more descriptive and meaningful.

Evaluation Criteria. The final column contains the criteria that will be used to evaluate the evidence as well as who will do the evaluating. The means of evaluating the evidence must also be stated. The type of criteria will vary with the type of learning objectives established and the evidence presented. Evaluators may be facilitators, peers, community experts, supervisors, and others who are considered qualified to judge the evidence. The numerous means of evaluating the evidence include the use of rating scales, descriptive commentaries, and evaluative reports. Learners should be involved in the design of the evaluation instruments that are used to judge and validate their evidence.

Advantages and Limitations

There are numerous advantages as well as limitations to using learning contracts. The primary advantages are the flexibility that the contract process offers to learners, the opportunity it provides in using preferred learning styles, the establishment of an appropriate pace of learning, and the notion that as learning needs change so can the contract learning objectives (O'Donnell & Caffarella, 1990). Contract learning places the responsibility and control of the learning with the learner. This reinforces the commitment, accountability, and motivation to follow though on the learning encounter (Smith, 1982). Learning contracts also assist learners in becoming more self-directed in the process of identifying learning needs and objectives, locating resources, planning learning activities, and becoming skilled at self-evaluation.

Learning contracts also have some limitations. Knowles (1986) suggests that contract learning is not suitable for all situations, particularly in learning situations that involve psychomotor skills or interpersonal skills, or in situations where the content is new and unfamiliar to the learners. Learning contracts also pose problems for learners who have dependent personalities and desire more structured learning activities. Closely related is the problem of reorienting learners toward being more independent and accepting control of their own learning as willingly as they do other aspects of their lives.

Brookfield (1986, p. 81) writes that "The ability to write contracts is a learned skill. . . . and it cannot be assumed that learners possess this innate ability." Therefore, facilitators need to provide some assistance to learners on planning and writing contracts before asking them to incorporate learning contracts into their educational activities. The learning contract process asks facilitators and learners to mutually and collaboratively be engaged in the learning encounter. The process requires learners to be risk takers and invites them to accept challenges that foster new intellectual, personal, and professional growth and development. Primary elements of the learning contract are its capability to enhance critical reflection throughout the process, the constant renegotiating of ideas, ways of reaching the learning objectives, and finally the realization of how this connects to the various aspects of their lives. The learning contract process allows for collaboration, challenge, critical reflection, and praxis to be incorporated into the educational encounter. As a result, contract learning seems to be most appropriate and consistent with the adult learning transactional process.

INQUIRY TEAMS

Enhancing collaboration, challenge, critical reflection, and praxis in action can also be realized through the use of inquiry teams. The most effective use of the inquiry team has been in graduate level courses when the size of the class has been larger than fifteen students. The larger group is divided into smaller groups of between three and eight participants. These smaller groups are then referred to as inquiry teams. The inquiry team method is a process whereby a group of learners addresses specific questions about a topic or elements of an issue and takes full control and responsibility for discovering answers or solutions to them. Ultimately, each inquiry team will be responsible for assisting in helping the larger group understand the information generated in the inquiry team.

The Planning Process

Knowles (1975) initially developed the concept of inquiry teams. The purpose of the method is to allow learners an opportunity to fully participate in the educational encounter. The process begins with the identification of learning needs and translating those needs into broad inquiry questions and learning objectives. For example, one broad inquiry question may be "What are the factors that contribute to lifelong learning in America?" Under this question five or six inquiry questions or learning objectives that relate to it may be identified. A class may generate four or five very broad areas of inquiry and identify specific learning objectives for each area. Once the class has identified the inquiry areas each participant can volunteer to work in a team that will address one broad area of inquiry. A class usually consists of approximately four inquiry teams.

Each inquiry team gets together and begins by introducing each team member. They exchange information about themselves such as addresses, telephone numbers, and what resources and experiences they can bring to the group that will aid in addressing the inquiry objectives. A considerable amount of time is spent on reviewing the objectives and their meanings. The facilitator during this time is available for consultation with each group to address any questions they may have and to offer some focus and direction to the activity. Groups are encouraged to review available resource material and to begin to delegate tasks among the members. After the division of responsibilities is done, each team member begins examining the resources (human and material) that will lead to some resolution to the questions or issues under consideration.

Inquiry teams spend between two and four weeks in team planning sessions. Between each planning session participants explore the resources directly related to their specific question or topic. Participants report back to the inquiry team each week what information has been generated toward the solution to the inquiry question. During this planning time exciting things begin to emerge. Learners begin to share information and resources, work collaboratively to find solutions and answers to questions, challenge held assumptions, and identify alternatives for addressing the tasks. It is in these planning sessions that learners find collaboration in learning. They have the opportunity to challenge one another, take risks, reflect on what information has been generated, and release their creative abilities and imaginations. From week to week during the planning process teams create a balance between critical reflection and the process of praxis in action.

Toward the end of the planning sessions teams are asked to identify strategies that can be used to present their inquiry questions or issues to the rest of the class. Each team usually has three to four sessions, approximately three hours per session, for the facilitation process. Surprisingly each team usually begins the process of planning the facilitation of the learning with some discussion on the philosophical orientation that they as a group hold toward the teaching and learning transaction. From this each team identifies what methods, techniques, and resources seem most appropriate. They are also asked to develop evaluation criteria and instruments that they can hand out at the end of each session. Evaluation forms are usually designed to provide information to the team on how helpful their session was to others in reaching an understanding of the issue at hand as well as how useful were the methods, strategies, handout materials, readings, and so forth. The evaluation data is used in the planning for the next week's session.

The Facilitation Process

Most inquiry teams are very creative in their approaches to the facilitation process. Some teams will have copies of articles, book chapters, lists of suggested readings, inventories, and other materials that they will provide to the class participants a week or so in advance of each facilitation session. Teams hold high expectations that each learner will have read the material before class and be ready to participate in the educational activity. Many teams incorporate role playing and other simulation exercises into the facilitation process as well as use critical incident exercises, case studies, and open discussion activities.

During the facilitation process by the inquiry team, the course facilitator becomes an active participant and learner. The facilitator may raise questions at appropriate times that have not been addressed by the team or offer some additional information or another perspective on the issue. The purpose of the facilitator is not to dominate the learning encounter but to help clarify and add to the body of information. Toward the end of each session the facilitator spends some time commenting and analyzing on the learning experience that has taken place. After class the inquiry team and the facilitator meet to discuss any concerns they experienced about the session and to discuss what changes they may want to make for the next week.

Benefits of Inquiry Teams

The inquiry team method has numerous advantages and benefits for adult learners. First and foremost is the advantage of working collaboratively in solving questions and issues of concern without the need to be competitive. Inquiry team efforts are evaluated on the basis of a team, not on individual performance. Each inquiry team seems to build into the process a natural means of solving conflict within the group, if it arises. The idea of contributing to the group in some significant way is more important than worrying about whether each member has contributed equally. In addition, inquiry teams grasp the idea and excitement of being independent and in control of the learning process. This allows the teams to be creative and free to take risks in how they will reach resolution of their tasks. Throughout the process individuals begin to construct open, caring, and trusting relationships. Members become friends that share personal and professional concerns, hopes, and dreams.

The inquiry method also helps learners to become more self-directing in their learning efforts. They hold the responsibility of identifying learning needs, locating appropriate resources, planning learning activities, and developing evaluation criteria and instruments. Inquiry teams members have an opportunity to facilitate adult learning before other adult learners within a real educational setting. This is perhaps the most exciting and meaningful experience for many individuals and the most terrifying for others, yet still rewarding (after it's over!).

The planning process contributes to a great deal of learning, although many learners do not realize how much they have learned independently in their pursuit for answers. Each planning meeting incorporates additional ideas, moments of reflection, and action strategies up to the time the inquiry team is ready to present its information to the entire class. During the facilitation process, the team assists the other learners in thinking critically about the questions and issues.

To incorporate the inquiry team method into the teaching and learning process, skill in group dynamics is necessary. Facilitators and learners must renegotiate their roles and functions. A vital first step is a careful explanation about these changing roles as well as about the rationale, purpose, and process of the inquiry method. Although this is time consuming, the potential for collaborative, challenging, reflective, and transforming learning is tremendous and very exciting.

CASE METHOD

In the case method a small group of participants, usually between six and twenty, is given information about a situation, either hypothetical or true, and asked to recommend actions to be taken. The group is asked to research the facts of the case, which are sometimes provided in class, and sometimes available only through diligent background research. From these facts group members make decisions or recommendations that could be implemented under the case description provided. This method is used in many graduate schools of business administration, law, social work, engineering, theology, and communications, but it may also be used appropriately in a variety of learning settings including community service agencies, adult education programs, management seminars, and staff and faculty development programs (Marsick, 1990). The goal of the case method is to promote action, growth, and development.

Necessary Conditions

The information presented in a case includes a statement of purpose or a description of the problem, background information, and factual information that would typically be available to the individuals involved in the decision-making process. Participants are usually provided only the background data. They must acquire any additional information independently. Depending upon the purposes established for using the case method, learners might be encouraged to read theories and hypotheses to guide them in reaching a decision. For example, if learners are asked to design a community development project they might need to learn about economic trends, the history of a community, and so forth. Although the benefits of the case method include collaborative learning, it can be conducted independently, depending upon the particular goals to be accomplished. Furthermore, it is entirely appropriate for instructors and colleagues to serve as resources in the process. The collaborative development of problem-solving strategies developed by students and facilitators can lead to a mutually rewarding experience.

The conditions for successful implementation of the case method include the selection of provoking cases and in-depth preparation by the facilitator and participants prior to the group discussion. While developing the case, participants will often acquire data that would not be available to them as an individual working alone or as a mere observer. The depth of data collection and the variety of perspectives from which it can be viewed often broaden a participant's perspective and result in decisions that otherwise might not have been considered viable by the participant.

Benefits

The case method enables participants to review information needed for critical decision making. Its benefits include promoting theoretical understanding and insight, inducing motivation and psychological involvement, and encouraging self-direction in learning (Romm & Mahler, 1986). Long term goals of the case method include the development of team spirit, smooth group interaction, and effective verbal and nonverbal communication. Participants should develop the ability to view a situation objectively and to make decisions that will be advantageous to the long term goals of the situation (or case) presented to them (Pigors & Pigors, 1987). By encouraging collaborative learning, participants enhance their critical reflectivity and interpersonal development.

Additional benefits of the case method include participants' enhanced reasoning skills. They are able to observe the inability of any individual to understand every aspect of a case—or even to think of every aspect of the case. The value of individual specialization is recognized in light of the benefits of collaborative efforts at decision making. Participants soon realize that other members of their group emphasized different aspects of the case. They also realize that their instructors or facilitators may not have the "right" answer. Finally, they realize that each problem has more than one reasonable solution.

Debriefing and Refining

After a case is completed the team presents it to the class or the group. Background information, procedures used to uncover significant facts, hypotheses generated and tested along the way, hazards anticipated and experienced, pleasant surprises experienced, and the final recommendations are all presented. The group hearing the case is encouraged to ask questions, to offer insights or other potential solutions to the problem, and to delve into the process used by the team. The discussion often includes a review of additional details that might have led to different recommendations, the human reactions likely to occur as a result of a decision, those human factors that ultimately determined the outcome, and the factors that are most likely to bring about the desired end to the case. If additional suggestions are made that might benefit the actions recommended, the team can use the information and reformulate its final set of recommendations. The recommendations are written up and presented to the facilitator and in many instances, to the individuals or groups actually represented in the study.

Analysis and Synthesis. It is through the discussion session that participants develop what Bondeson (1981) calls "philosophical skills" or skills transmitted through philosophy. By having a critical discussion of the debriefing session, two modes of philosophical activity are enhanced—analysis and synthesis. As with students of philosophy, participants in the case method must practice analysis through the examination of a certain point of view to first,

> determine precisely what is being said, what terms are being used, and how those terms are defined. A great deal of work may be required to interpret statements and clarify the view under discussion. Once a view is clearly stated, the next task is to understand the data, arguments, and other kinds of supporting evidence. (Bondeson, 1981, p. 363)

Bondeson suggests that argumentation is a matter of skill which is learned only through practice. Philosophical synthesis occurs when arguments are weighed against each other. Evidence is accumulated and there is the balancing of views, of thesis and antithesis. All this requires skill in judgment, being able to think through all arguments and then, after critical reflection, being able to put them together into a synthetic whole. According to Bondeson, analysis must precede synthesis. "The details of experience, the experience of individual cases, and the careful analysis of concepts and arguments are the materials out of which the larger syntheses are constructed" (p. 364).

Role of the Facilitator

Facilitators of the case method should be aware of the thought processes that transpire as people collect, analyze, and synthesize data. They should also be aware of the pitfalls that can occur as a result of inadequate preparation or a lack of indepth perspective when using the case study. If individuals do not acquire adequate information during independent study, cases are likely to fall short.

The group may therefore be unable to reach a reasonable solution and the facilitator must regroup and lead a beneficial discourse. The facilitator should keep the discussion moving, acknowledge the contributions of participants, and highlight significant points. It is also important to maintain students' interest in the case as well as the goals of the course or workshop. Finally, the facilitator should be sure that the final position taken is well-reasoned and that it entails a definite line of action (Bernstein, 1976).

CRITICAL INCIDENT

The earliest and most systematic description of the critical incident was developed by John C. Flannagan (1954) who described an incident as an observable human action that is sufficiently complete in itself to permit inferences to be made about the person whose actions are being observed. The approach is useful when studying specific incidents of effective or ineffective behavior as related to a designed activity. The outcome of the technique is to provide an objective, factual description of such behaviors. To conduct a critical incident exercise the facilitator prompts participants to identify an incident that was particularly meaningful to them. Instructions are given on the type of incident to be identified and individuals are asked to write one or two paragraphs describing the particulars of the event. Brookfield (1987) suggests that specific instructions might include these elements: a description of the situation on which you are reporting, "(1) when and where it occurred, (2) who was involved (roles and job titles rather than personal identities may be given here), and (3) what it was about the incident that was so significant as to cause a problem" (p. 97). Other questions that can be considered are, what did you do, and what did your supervisor (or other significant player) say or do?

Data Collection and Interpretation

The typical steps included in a critical incident data gathering strategy include the following: determining the purpose of the activity, developing the plans and procedures for collecting factual incidents related to an activity, collecting objective and relevant data through interviews or written records, analyzing the data in a way that makes it practical and useful, and interpreting and reporting the results of the activity. The reporting phase should include descriptions of possible biases and implications inherent in the four previous steps (Cohen & Smith, 1976). Although the procedures used in the critical incident technique have been altered over the years, it is important that two principles be stressed. First, the reporting of observable behaviors is far more beneficial than interpreting the motives behind behaviors, and second, only those behaviors that make a significant contribution to the activity should be reported.

Critical incidents represent only raw data and do not necessarily offer solutions to problems. However, by tabulating multiple observations it should be possible to describe the critical concerns and assumptions of respondents. Brookfield (1987) suggests that by collecting written responses to specific instructions a facilitator can assess the anxieties or difficulties that learners or workers are experiencing. Meaningful educational activities could then be designed to respond to the real-life needs of participants. Critical incidents can assist learners with analyzing their experiential learning, self-directed learning, or their interpersonal communication skills. Through the critical incident technique, learners can make critical assessments of their assumptions, thoughts, and actions and begin to consider alternatives to them.

MENTORING

Although an abundance of research and literature on mentoring exists, Merriam (1983), in her critical review of the literature on mentoring, suggested that no agreed upon definition of mentoring could be found. For our purpose, mentoring will be defined as a powerful emotional and passionate interaction whereby the mentor and protégé experience personal, professional, and intellectual growth and development. It is a unique one-to-one teaching and learning method that incorporates the basic elements of the transactional process—collaboration, challenge, critical reflection, and praxis. Mentoring, as a tool to enhance learning, can be found in a variety of settings such as business and industry (Bova, 1987; Kram, 1985; Phillips-Jones, 1982), higher education (Daloz, 1986, 1987, 1990), and public schools (Wilcox, 1987). It has long played an important part in understanding the development and growth of men and women (Belenky, Clinchy, Goldberger, & Tarule, 1986; Daloz, 1986; Kegan, 1982; Levinson et al., 1978; Sheehy, 1976). Mentoring is a powerful transformative process that allows and encourages individuals to reinterpret their personal, professional, and political environments and to search out alternative ways of thinking and acting. It is a method that insists that learners confront and wrestle with differing viewpoints and perspectives if intellectual growth, change, and development are to occur (Daloz, 1988).

Mentor and Protégé Roles

The literature describes the role of a mentor in various ways. For some a mentor is a role model, advocate, sponsor, counselor, challenger, developer of skills and intellect, listener, host, and balancer. Daloz (1986) suggests that a mentor is a guide. The guide helps move a protégé along the journey toward discovering and examining newfound intellectual territory. A mentor shares the dream or vision of the learner and assists in its promotion.

What are the roles of the learner or protégé who enters into a mentoring relationship? The primary role must be that of a risk taker—one who will wander into unfamiliar territory with the hope of finding new and exciting intellectual discoveries. Such a person accepts the risks of commitment to new learning and of confrontation, critical analysis, and evaluation of the journey. This person seeks independence, desires to see things in new ways, and accepts challenges that will lead to adult development and growth. The protégé is also a separator and a connector. There must be a willingness to separate the old ways of thinking and acting from the new and to critically reflect upon what this means within the context of one's life. Being a connector means to relate or connect new information and discoveries to life experiences and roles and to find this connection educationally transforming.

Functions of Mentoring

A mentoring relationship should result in growth for both mentor and protégé, although Daloz (1986) suggests that ultimately "the trip belongs, after all, to the traveler, not the guide . . ." (p. 33). It is the purpose of a mentoring relationship to unveil new perspectives and new ways of thinking and acting. Mentoring should assist learners in becoming critical thinkers.

What then are the functions of the mentoring relationship that

will help bring about adult development and growth, critical thinking, critical reflection, and the incorporation of the process of
praxis? Daloz (1986, 1987, 1990) provides various strategies to
help guide learners toward these ends. He suggests three ways mentors can enhance growth—they support, they challenge, and they
provide vision. His work will serve as a basis for the next paragraphs in detailing such strategies and functions.

Support. Daloz (1990) writes that to "support a student is to
affirm that person's essential integrity, to say that no matter what is
to come, she is fundamentally OK" (p. 209). Support means to
engender trust and courage within the relationship so growth can
occur. Several primary elements of mentorship can provide this
support. One such element is listening, perhaps the most powerful
and valuable talent that a good mentor can possess (Daloz, 1987).
Listening is more than hearing what is being said. It means "actively
engaging with the student's world and attempting to experience it
from the inside" (Daloz, 1986, p. 215). Another element is that of
providing structure. Depending upon the developmental level, some
learners will need a high degree of structure to make them feel safe
and supportive. However, this dependency should move toward
more independence and less structure once the learners realize that
they possess the ability and intellect to be more independent in the
learning encounter. The learner will make it quite clear that the time
has come to be more independent. Active listening will make the
mentor aware of such time. A mentor also expresses positive expectations and an affirmation that some sort of movement toward
growth is essential. This suggests that the learner is competent and
capable of change. The mentor dwells on what is positive and good
and not on what is wrong. Mentors also provide support to the
learner by being an advocate and a translator of the unknown
system (an academic or business setting, for example) in which the
learning is occurring. Because mentors are experienced in the setting
and know the "ins and outs," providing support throughout this
unknown journey can be a welcome gift to the learner. Support also
comes by sharing in a timely manner something about ourselves as
mentors. Mentorship is a highly personal interaction and to gain the
feelings of trust, care, and genuine concern about the experience,
individuals involved in the mentoring process must be willing to be
open, honest, and personal. Openness allows each person to be seen
as an individual through self-disclosure. When supportive activities

are present in a mentoring relationship, learners begin to feel special and important. They gain a willingness and sense of freedom to explore new ways of thinking and acting.

Challenge. The second major strategy that the mentor utilizes to promote growth and development is through challenge. Challenging raises the questions about the status quo and invites the learner to entertain alternative ways of thinking and acting. The first element of challenge is to set tasks that will help the protégé not only to gain knowledge but also to critically reflect on its meaning and implications. Challenging tasks serve as a mechanism to view the world from new perspectives. Setting tasks should be done thoughtfully to bring about change, growth, and intellectual development.

Another function that is central to challenge is the provision for discussion. As Daloz (1990) suggests, a mentor provides an alternative voice. Through discussion mentor and learner explore alternative ways of viewing various phenomena or problems. It is the task of the mentor to understand the way the learner is thinking and to raise questions about it. Questioning is important because it can lead to a better understanding of the assumptions that the learner holds as being "right," "wrong," "good," "bad," and so on. It helps to identify what the learner really believes. Discussion can challenge learners to see both sides of the issue before taking a stand or position (Daloz, 1986). Another purpose behind the function of challenge is to encourage hypothetical thinking. The "what if" approach to assumptions can help learners understand different perspectives and views. A mentor calls on learners to use their imaginations to picture some alternative form of reality. Finally, mentors challenge learners through the setting of high standards as well as through the development of a mechanism for them to construct their own set of expectations. "Students' growth ultimately depends on their developing the ability to look dispassionately at their own performance, their own answers to their own questions, and decide for themselves how they've done" (Daloz, 1986, p. 229). Mentoring is about helping adults learn how to learn, not how to be taught.

Vision. The third major function of the mentor is to help learners identify their own visions. Daloz (1986) states that "Vision, in its broadest sense, is the field on which the dialectical game between the old self and the new can be played; it is the context that hosts both support and challenge in the service of transformation" (p. 230). Modeling is the first of the elements in developing a vision.

It is a powerful element but the focus of modeling should not be on the desire of the learner to be like the mentor. The endeavor should rather be one of challenging learners to transcend themselves and to fully obtain and reach their highest aspirations. According to Daloz (1986) "What we model for our students is not our knowledge but our curiosity, the journey, not the destination" (p. 232). Closely related to modeling is the notion of offering a map to learners that will help them see more clearly their journey or destination. Asking appropriate questions about their aspirations, dreams, desires, learning needs, and so forth can help the mentor design this map. Learners can begin to see where their journey is headed and begin to take control over the process of transforming this journey into reality.

Daloz (1986, 1987, 1990) suggests that the way language is used can help shape the learners' reality. The "use of common language can be a powerful way in which mentors maintain a connection with their students while helping them to transform the meaning of their words" (Daloz, 1987, p. 37). When learners use unqualified language as "good," "true," "always," and so on, mentors should help learners see the relativity and contingency of such language. By understanding this and implementing alternative language, mentors and learners can begin to explore new meaning to the language that is used and to see the contextuality of it for their lives and the potential it holds for growth and development. Finally, the mentor provides vision by providing a mirror that allows learners to see themselves the way they are and gives them new alternatives for viewing the world about them. Seeing several different perspectives expands the scope of their thinking. It calls into question the habitual givens accepted and encourages the alteration of held assumptions, values, ideas, and actions. Learners begin to see the outcomes of critical reflection and the implications for new development. Providing a mirror begins the development of critically aware thinkers.

Mentoring is an appropriate method that incorporates the essential elements of the adult learning transactional process. A meaningful and rewarding mentoring relationship depends upon collaboration that can be highly emotional. If a mentoring relationship is to promote growth and development, elements of challenge and risk taking must be present. However, caring and understanding must be the guiding principles to such challenge and risk taking. The process of critical reflection becomes apparent when the learners show evidence of understanding the contextuality of their learning and how it affects their personal, professional, social, and political lives. Finally, the process of praxis is present, whether observable or not, when learners take action on their critical reflective activities and such activities promote the development of new perspectives. Mentoring is a powerful method to enhance the one-to-one teaching and learning transaction. It is a process that can promote significant learning and growth.

REFERENCES

Belenky, M., Clinchy, B., Goldberger, N., & Tarule, J. (1986). *Women's ways of knowing: The development of self, voice, and mind.* New York: Basic Books.

Bergevin, P., Morris, D., & Smith, R. (1963). *Adult education procedures: A handbook of tested patterns for effective participation.* New York: Seabury.

Bernstein, H. (1976). *Manual for teaching* (rev. ed.). New York: Author and Cornell University.

Bondeson, W. (1981). Philosophy. In A. Chickering (Ed.), *The modern American college* (pp. 355–369). San Francisco: Jossey-Bass.

Bova, B. (1987). Mentoring as a learning experience. In V. Marsick (Ed.), *Learning in the workplace* (pp. 119–133). London: Croom Helm.

Brookfield, S. (1985). Discussion as an effective educational method. In S. Rosenblum (Ed.), *Involving adults in the educational process* (pp. 55–67). New Directions for Continuing Education, no. 26. San Francisco: Jossey-Bass.

Brookfield, S. (1986). *Understanding and facilitating adult learning.* San Francisco: Jossey-Bass.

Brookfield, S. (1987). *Developing critical thinkers.* San Francisco: Jossey-Bass.

Brookfield, S. (1990). Discussion. In M. W. Galbraith (Ed.), *Adult learning methods: A guide for effective instruction* (pp. 187–204). Malabar, FL: Krieger.

Cohen, A., & Smith, R. (1976). *The critical incident in growth groups: Theory and technique.* LaJolla: University Associates.

Daloz, L. (1986). *Effective teaching and mentoring.* San Francisco: Jossey-Bass.

Daloz, L. (1987). Martha meets her mentor. *Change, 19*(4), 35–37.

Daloz, L. (1988). Beyond tribalism: Renaming the good, the true, and the beautiful. *Adult Education Quarterly, 38*(4), 234–241.

Daloz, L. (1990). Mentorship. In M. W. Galbraith (Ed.), *Adult learning methods: A guide for effective instruction* (pp. 205–224). Malabar, FL: Krieger.

Flannagan, J. (1954). The critical incident technique. *Psychological Bulletin, 51*(4), 327–358.

Galbraith, M. W. (Ed.). (1990). *Adult learning methods: A guide for effective instruction*. Malabar, FL: Krieger.

Houle, C. (1972). *The design of education*. San Francisco: Jossey-Bass.

Kegan, R. (1982). *The evolving self*. Cambridge: Harvard University Press.

Knowles, M. (1975). *Self-directed learning: A guide for learners and teachers*. Chicago: Follett.

Knowles, M. (1984). *The adult learner: A neglected species* (3rd. ed.). Houston: Gulf.

Knowles, M. (1986). *Using learning contracts*. San Francisco: Jossey-Bass.

Knox, A. (1986). *Helping adults learn*. San Francisco: Jossey-Bass.

Kolb, D. (1981). Learning styles and disciplinary differences. In A. Chickering (Ed.), *The modern American college* (pp. 232–255). San Francisco: Jossey-Bass.

Kram, K. (1985). *Mentoring at work: Developmental relationships in organizational life*. Glenview: Scott, Foresman and Company.

Levinson, D., Darrow, C., Klein, E., Levinson, M., & McKee, B. (1978). *The seasons of a man's life*. New York: Ballantine.

Lindeman, E. (1926). *The meaning of adult education*. New York: New Republic.

Marsick, V. (1990). Case study. In M. W. Galbraith (Ed.), *Adult learning methods: A guide for effective instruction* (pp. 225–246). Malabar, FL: Krieger.

Merriam, S. (1983). Mentors and protégés: A critical review of the literature. *Adult Education Quarterly, 33*(3), 161–173.

Morgan, B., Holmes, C., & Bundy, C. (1976). *Methods in adult education* (3rd. ed.). Danville: Interstate Printers and Publishers.

O'Donnell, J., & Caffarella, R. (1990). Learning contracts. In M. W. Galbraith (Ed.), *Adult learning methods: A guide for effective instruction* (pp. 133–160). Malabar, FL: Krieger.

Paterson, R. (1970). The concept of discussion: A philosophical approach. *Studies in adult education,* 2(1), 28–50.

Phillips-Jones, L. (1982). *Mentors and protégés.* New York: Arbor House.

Pigors, P., & Pigors, F. (1987). Case method. In R. Craig (Ed.), *Training and development handbook* (pp. 414–429). New York: McGraw-Hill.

Romm, T., & Mahler, S. (1986). A three dimensional model for using case studies in the academic classroom. *Higher Education, 15,* 677–696.

Schön, D. (1983). *The reflective practitioner.* New York: Basic Books.

Sheehy, G. (1976). *Passages: Predictable crises of adult life.* New York: E. P. Dutton.

Smith, R. (1982). *Learning how to learn.* Chicago: Follett.

Wilcox, K. (1987). Training master teachers to mentor. In V. Marsick (Ed.), *Learning in the workplace* (pp. 134–148). London: Croom Helm.

CHAPTER 6

Technology for Teaching and Learning Improvement

CONSTANCE C. BLACKWOOD
BARBARA A. WHITE

By the end of the twentieth century, education will have been significantly impacted by the movement of American culture from an agricultural and industrial society to an "information society." As a result, contemporary educators will have to devise strategies and implement delivery methods that make information accessible to individuals in the workplace, during leisure, or in the more general pursuit of human potential. To accomplish such a task will require a clear understanding of the nature of information, of the technologies by which information is structured, of the intellectual strategies employed to interpret information, and of the sociocultural milieu created by a technological environment. In addition, the educator will need to recognize the role played by technology in facilitating the teaching-learning transaction and the contribution by technology in reaching out to the learner irrespective of time and distance.

Factors affected by and/or affecting technology have included distance education, microcomputer-based learning, instructional design considerations, learning styles, open learning systems, and the interpretation of what is meant by lifelong learning. For example, in the case of distance education the technology is more than an adjunct to the instructional process; it is the main organizational system linking student and teacher. Garrison (1987) notes that computer-assisted instruction (CAI) has the capability to cope with the diverse needs and characteristics of the adult learner. In addition, CAI can (a) provide alternative means of reaching goals, (b) provide flexibility for the learner in controlling and pacing the learning experience, and (c) provide for independent and self-directed learning. Of importance to the learner, CAI can do all of this in a secure, private, and patient manner.

With respect to instructional design considerations, it has been suggested that educators must not be preoccupied with technology, but instead should see it as a vehicle of delivery that can structure messages in differing and unique ways. "It is the message and the learner that must be of paramount concern in the selection of technological delivery systems" (Garrison, 1987, p. 47). With regard to learning styles, technology has provided access to learning where it previously did not exist, but it also has provided the potential to improve the quality of learning support by individualizing learning and recognizing preferred learning styles. And, an open learning system is very much learner-centered and makes use of traditional classrooms and societal settings, as well as using a variety of instructional methods that may or may not be technologically based. Finally, to operationalize the concept of lifelong learning, delivery of education is distributed along a lifelong continuum with an emphasis toward the electronic delivery of educational opportunities.

In presenting a theory/research-to-practice approach to the facilitation of adult learning, educators of adults need to have a clear understanding of how educational technology can contribute to reaching educational goals and objectives. Certainly, the use of a particular instructional medium or technology becomes essential to the accomplishment of many objectives. Educational technology should form an integral part of the instructional plan and play a role in facilitating the desired intellectual processes and outcomes.

The purpose of this chapter is to provide a discussion of the use of educational technology as an enhancement to the teaching and learning transaction. With this in mind, educational technology is defined as the scientific application of knowledge and hardware to teaching and learning (Garrison, 1987). Technology is defined as any means, form, or vehicle by which instruction is formatted, stored, and delivered to learners (Schwen, 1977); technology is also defined as the integration of both hardware and knowledge.

A secondary purpose is the presentation of information identifying technologies which work most effectively in combination with selected domains of learning and the educational setting. Third, the chapter includes a discussion of (a) a variety of available technologies which feature an interactive component, (b) technologies which are considered to be accessible, and (c) instances in which the identified technologies are most effective. A final section addresses the future of instructional technology in adult education. The underlying assumption of this chapter is that technology can be designed to be collaborative for the teaching and learning transaction.

THE TEACHING AND LEARNING TRANSACTION

Educational technology should be considered within the complex interactions of any teaching and learning transaction. All aspects of the transaction need to be taken into consideration, including an understanding of the structure of the content, the variety and implications of learning styles, and the impact of the total environment on the learner. Often, the total teaching and learning system must be designed and coordinated with the many needs of the adult "distant learner" as the focus. For example, television courses cannot merely be added on to a system, but require a reconceptualization of who the learners are and what they need in order to benefit from the interaction (Meierhenry, 1981).

Bradford (1958) stated two assumptions regarding the teaching and learning transaction. One is that this process is a human transaction involving the teacher, learner, and learning group in a set of dynamic interrelationships. The second assumption is that teachers and learners engage in a complex process of exploration and diagnosis. The process includes (a) needs for and resistances to learning and change, (b) experimentation and fact finding, and (c) testing and planning for the utilization of learning and change in the life of the individual. Figure 6.1 shows the more traditional teaching and learning transaction in which the teacher is identified as the disseminator of knowledge and the learner as the "passive" recipient. Figure 6.2 illustrates the interactivity that is an integral force within the adult teaching and learning transaction. The illustration

TEACHER ———▶ STUDENT

Figure 6.1 The traditional teaching and learning transaction.

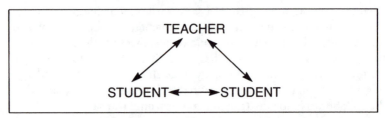

Figure 6.2 Interactivity within the teaching and learning transaction.

reaffirms the direction of teaching and learning theory for adult learning in which active feedback is a critical element in the educational experience (Travers, 1982).

Complementing the interactive aspect is the emphasis placed on the collaborative or facilitative methods incorporated into the learning situation. Adult education literature supports the collaborative mode as the most effective method for teaching adults. Consensus is that curriculum, the type of educational agency delivering the program, the type of student to be recruited, and the maturity of the students must also be taken into consideration.

EDUCATIONAL TECHNOLOGY AS A CONTRIBUTOR TO EFFECTIVE INSTRUCTION

Knowles (1983) predicted that by the end of the twentieth century, most educational services will be delivered electronically. Delivery would include teleconferencing, cable and satellite television, computer networks, and other means to be discovered—provided that educators of adults learn how to use the technology in congruence with principles of adult learning. Knowles further stated that learning is most effective when the learners are engaged interactively in a process of inquiry. This could be accomplished in two ways: (1) by having interaction between the learner and the program such as demonstrated by the use of computer-assisted instruction, and (2) by having interaction among the learners and between them as a group and the program, as provided in the use of two-way audio or video teleconferencing and cable or satellite television programming. Knowles (1983) identified key features in the use of technology:

1. Programs involving instructional technology must be organized around the acquisition of the knowledge, skills, understandings, attitudes, and values that are applicable to performing the life tasks they are concerned with.

2. Instructional programs need to provide for a wide range of options in learning because of the differences among learners in terms of experiential backgrounds, readiness to learn, motivation, learning styles, developmental stages, and pace of learning.

3. Programs incorporating instructional technology need to allow for decision-making opportunities by the learners in regard to what they are going to learn, when they will learn it, and how they are going to verify that they have met the desired objective.

Pratt (1987) suggested that when considering the use of technology within education, the effectiveness of the instruction depends on several interacting factors. These include the nature of the content to be learned, the nature of the technology used, the time available, the cost of delivery, the quality of the learning experience, and the ability to respond to differences among learners.

Implementing Educational Technology

A major question when considering any technology for the delivery of instruction must be "What type of learning will it promote and how will that shape our thinking about instruction?" The test of effectiveness of educational technology lies not in the form but in its ability to serve specific instructional functions. Coursework for classroom delivery is usually planned with two main elements in mind, the teacher and the learner. The educational technology must be compatible with the instructional methods and strategies employed. The underlying assumptions for adult education should not, however, be compromised by the choice of technology. According to Burnham and Seamon (1987), "Decisions about how to educate should be driven by desired learning outcomes and not by convenient or untested devices and systems" (p. 11).

Ely (1988) has identified six educational technology-based elements that tend to make programs more successful:

1. Elements that meet critical educational needs

2. Elements oriented toward the individual learner rather than the teacher

3. Elements that are cost-effective

4. Elements that have relatively simple and available delivery systems

5. Elements that emphasize the design of the system

6. Elements that are more often involved in training than in education

Less successful program elements include:

1. Confused goals

2. Emphasis on the medium

3. Resistance to change

4. Lack of support systems

5. Lack of skills

6. Expense

Possible reasons for program failures include "technophobia," an inhibition of human contact, disruption of legal or economic status, or lack of appropriate designs and information. Other reasons for failure include technology that doesn't work reliably, other media which may be better suited, lack of local production ability, and the absence of standardization.

Educational Technology and the Learning Process

Gagné (1965) defined learning as a change in human disposition or capability which can be retained, and which is not simply ascribable to the process of growth. The type of change called *learning* is identified as a change in behavior and the inference of learning is made by comparing what behavior was possible before the individual was placed in the "learning situation" and what behavior is exhibited after such exposure. The changes may be in performance as well as capabilities. Elements critical to both situations include (a) learner, (b) the events that stimulate the learner's senses, and (c) the action that results from the stimulation and subsequent activity.

> A learning event, then, takes place when the stimulus situation affects the learner in such a way that his performance changes from a time before being in that situation to a time after being in it. The change in performance is what leads to the conclusion that learning has occurred. (Gagné, 1965, p. 6)

An important point is that these learning conditions must be carefully planned before the learning situation itself is entered into by the student.

The identification of conditions affecting learning obviously has some definite implications for education and educational practices. One such implications is found in the function of instruction, defined as arranging the conditions of learning that are *external* to the learner. Sometimes instruction is predesigned, as in the case of computer-assisted instruction; other times instruction is extemporaneously designed by the teacher.

The mode of instruction involves the resources for learning which may include traditional instructional media such as oral and printed communication. Electronic delivery systems include electronic print-base information, two-way audio teleconferencing, two-way video teleconferencing interactive video, or two-way "talkback" instructional television. The choice of instructional delivery is a matter of aiming for the most efficient plan for generating the proper conditions for learning.

The question becomes one, therefore, of how should instruction be designed? Four major assumptions from the instructional development literature provide a base for planning and designing instruction for the teaching and learning transaction. First, the instruction must be for the individual. Second, the design must incorporate phases that are both immediate and long-range. Third, the design of the instruction should be systematic in nature. And fourth, the designing of the instruction, and therefore the inclusion of the instructional strategy and *mode of delivery*, must be based upon knowledge of how human beings learn. "Materials for instruction need to reflect not simply what their author knows, but also how the student is intended to learn such knowledge" (Gagné & Briggs, 1974, p. 6).

Category/ Definition	Performance Objective Example	Suggested Mode
Intellectual Skills Capabilities that make the individual competent	Discriminate Identify Classify	Audiotape/print-base Instructional TV Interactive video Video cassette Computer assisted instruction (CAI) Videotex Audiotex
Cognitive Strategies Capabilities that govern individual's own learning, remembering, and thinking behavior	Generate solution to higher order rule using problem solving	Audio teleconferencing Interactive video Computer simulation Computer assisted instruction (CAI) Videotex Audiotex
Verbal Information Information which we have learned in school, in part for the course only, and in part the kind of knowledge we are expected to be able to recall as adults	List Recite State Summarize (in own words)	Interactive video Electronic print Audio cassette Audio teleconferencing Audio/data transmission Audiotex Videotex
Motor Skills Another type of capability we expect people to learn as part of formal schooling	Execute	Computer simulation Interactive video
Attitudes "Affective domain"; attitudes toward things, persons, and situations	Choose Select	Audiotape Audio teleconferencing Video teleconferencing Computer simulation Interactive video

Figure 6.3 Categories of performance objectives by category, definition, example, and suggested technology.

142

One approach used in the design of instruction is to work backward from the expected outcome. The initial step, however, is to identify the capabilities to be established by the instruction and, having categorized performance objectives, to identify the expected learning outcomes. Categories of objectives leading to learning outcomes include: intellectual skills, cognitive strategies, verbal information, motor skills, and attitudes. The matrix represented by Figure 6.3 describes each of the areas by category, definition, example, and appropriate educational technology.

For the purpose of this chapter, the assumption underlying the following section is that consideration must be given to the conditions affecting the learning of intellectual skills, noted by Gagné (1967) as of central importance in formal and informal educational environments. For example, the category of intellectual skills provides to the educator the instructional process and the selection of interactive instructional delivery modes most appropriate for the learning situation.

Intellectual skills can be categorized on a dimension of complexity. Gagné (1977) suggests the following as ranging from the less complex levels to greater complexity: discrimination, concepts, rules, and problem solving. The dilemma for the educator of adults is the selection of the most appropriate delivery mechanism (i.e., educational technology) for an interactive teaching and learning transaction. For example, which of the educational technologies could be used most effectively to facilitate rule learning while taking into consideration the assumptions underlying adult learning (i.e., self-direction, immediate application, readiness to learn, and the role played by experience in learning)?

INTERACTIVE EDUCATIONAL TECHNOLOGIES

The challenge is to develop or adapt instructional tools compatible with the participation of the learners. Kester and Gueulette (1981) suggest that "such participation requires interaction between the learner and the learning experience" (p. 7). "Interactive media" may require that the learner interact with the medium, not just react to it, through one of many forms: writing, verbalizing, manipulating something, or competing or cooperating with other learners. The concept of interactivity may be taken one step further by noting that media must go beyond the tutorial mode to one in which the student must make decisions about which tests to perform, which facts to investigate, and which calculations to make. It is only through this process that the learner becomes central to the learning experiences and the instructional devices become interactive. A different perspective presented by Heaney (1976) suggests that an interactive medium facilitates interaction between persons. Interactive media becomes a concept, not just a type of media.

Learners and educators must implement the use of educational technology creatively and imaginatively to ensure that the learner is central to the process. The mode of delivery becomes the means by which the learner, learners, and the instructor interact with each other. In order to accomplish an effective implementation and use of educational technology, educators of adults must have a familiarity with existing and future interactive technologies. Several guiding principles should be considered when organizing and implementing educational technologies:

1. Technologies should be selected with a firm understanding of how they could and should be used.

2. To be effective, the technology must be an integrated instructional component and not an afterthought.

3. Technology should be used to fill identified instructional needs, not just because it is sophisticated and state of the art.

4. Faculty should be involved in making decisions about educational technology.

5. The organization set up to oversee technological resources should see its primary mission as the support of instruction.

6. To be effective, educational technology should be viewed as a means to an end, as opposed to an end in itself.

The Electronic Technology Task Force Report (1985), representing the application of electronic technologies to the National Extension Service, provides examples of interactive educational technologies. The four major categories reviewed in this chapter, excerpted from the report, include electronic print-base selected technologies and audio, video, and data delivery modes. An emphasis has been placed on examples of electronic technologies which facilitate interactivity in the learning process. Each figure provides an opportunity to identify with the purposes of the educational experience (information delivery, education delivery, problem solving) and to review advantages and disadvantages of the selected technology.

Print-base Electronic Technology

This technology refers to captioned television and video text services used in delivering textual information to the public as well as to the application of electronic technologies to the traditional text media, including newspapers, magazines, pamphlets, publications, and newsletters. Expanded transmission speeds and increased processing power enable more and more textual material to be delivered directly to the consumer via computer display. Examples of this technology are electronic mail, informational database retrieval systems, and teletext. Figure 6.4 provides an overview of the features of print-base electronic technology based on the purpose of the delivery system (i.e., information, education, or problem solving).

Electronic Teletraining Technologies

Currently, teletraining technologies are becoming increasingly popular as they reduce the time and expense of staff travel and reach adult learners in remote locations. These technologies also have the potential to enhance the training of larger numbers of learners than would be possible in a more traditional manner. Categories of teletraining technologies noted in Figure 6.5 include audio and audio-graphic technology, audiovisual with an emphasis on the use of telephone lines, and full-motion video represented by a variety of delivery modes. The examples identified in Figure 6.5 and on the following pages provide an overview of potential interactive audio, video, and data systems which can enhance the facilitation of the teaching and learning transaction.

Telephone Dial Access

The telephone is becoming an increasingly important delivery mechanism as dial-in access to recorded messages is an economical way to deliver information. Message systems that convert text to voice provide an avenue for the learner to retrieve problem-solving information and expand the usefulness of the telephone. Telephone

Features of Print-base Electronic Technology	Information Delivery	Education Delivery	Problem Solving
Advantages	Information selected by audience Updated easily Storage and warehousing reduced Timely	Audiences targeted Product controlled Updated easily Storage and warehousing reduced	Responsive to audience needs Audiences targeted Product controlled Easily updated Storage and warehousing reduced
Disadvantages	Special handling required Telephone and computer costs Limited graphics	Special handling required Telephone and computer costs	Use limited by medium
Best Uses	Timely information updates Limited print orders	Procedures Description	Simple problems Large audiences

Figure 6.4 Features of electronic print-base technology relative to use in an information, educational, or problem-solving learning environment.

lines can deliver a variety of digital data to the learner's home with the data processed by a microcomputer, print, or displayed as video programs via television. In addition, technological advances combining radio, computers, and digital voice transmission improve the capability of mobile radio telephones in vehicles. Figure 6.6 provides information about telephone dial access as a potential interactive mechanism for facilitating learning.

Category	Technology	Delivery Mode
Audio and Audio- Graphic: One or two-way telephone transmission	Dial-up access via telephone	Direct dial to instructor or 900 service for telelecture
	Dial-up teleconferencing Meet-me bridges	Operator-assisted Linked lines leased from private companies providing operator assistance that provides operator or direct dial
	Dedicated networks	Hard-wire lines that permanently connect all training sites
	Slides or overheads	Mail or courier
Audiovisual: Two-way telephone plus use of visuals	Electronic blackboard, whiteboard, table or pen that sends drawings, etc., made on a pressure-sensitive slate to computer monitors at distant sites	Telephone lines
	Slowscan or freeze-frame transmission that sends still pictures	Telephone lines
Full-motion Video: One- or two-way live or taped moving images	Instructional Television Fixed Service (ITFS)	Special frequencies received at specified sites by a frequency converter
	Television	Satellite by transmitting digital and receiving analog or digital signals
	Television	Microwave
	Videotape	Mail or satellite
	Interactive video	Computer and video tape player combined
	Compressed video	Transmission of visual images via telephone lines

Figure 6.5 Overview of teletraining technologies.

147

Features of Telephone Dial Access	Information Delivery	Education Delivery	Problem Solving
Advantages	Good access Convenient Number of messages unlimited Large audiences reached Information localized	Good access Number of messages unlimited	Good access Responsive Localized to area
Disadvantages	Limited audience selection Preparation time for script recording	Limited duration of messages Costly Specialized staff needed	Use limited by medium
Best Uses	Simple content Timely information Routine information Delivery outside office hours Short (1–3 minute messages)	Simple content Timely information Routine information Delivery outside office hours Tapes up to 20 minutes in length	Simple content Timely information Use outside office hours

Figure 6.6 Features of electronic telephone dial-up access relative to use in an information, educational, or problem-solving learning environment.

Electronic Audio Technology

Audio tapes and cassettes have been used extensively as a delivery mechanism in context areas such as foreign languages and music education. Correspondence courses have incorporated audio cassettes with print-base support materials allowing for some learner independence and interaction. The use of a delivery system with both audio and visual components appears, however, to be more effective instructionally. Currently, one- and/or two-way audio teleconferencing is being widely used in an informational and educational context to deliver programs and coursework to a previously identified audience. Supplemental materials are very important when using audio teleconferencing, however, as all participants should have the same visual cues organized in the most convenient manner. Figure 6.7 provides an overview of audio teleconferencing features which may or may not enhance the teaching and learning transaction.

Educational Video Technology

The broad category of instructional television includes a variety of electronic technologies whose common information display mechanism is the television monitor. For example, with visual impact desirable, one- or two-way video teleconferencing provides full motion visuals to support information and educational delivery. More advanced transmission modes for video include satellite transponders, microwave transmission, underground fiber-optic strands, and the telephone lines. Examples of educational video technology include videotape and tape players, interactive video which includes the video equipment plus a computer, one- and/or two-way video teleconferencing, compressed video, computer-generated text and graphic images on video, and computer-controlled videodisk players. Figure 6.8 provides features of educational video in a learning environment.

Data Transmission

As telecommunications are converted to digital format, the computer plays an increasingly important role in the information society. The computer can switch, process, and convert digital information streams from one medium to another. It converts text to voice and stores voice messages. The computer also can digitize and store video signals.

The personal computer can serve as the controller or manager of several components of a distance delivery system. It has the capability to communicate with remote sources of information, re-

Features of Electronic Audio Tele-conferencing	Information Delivery	Education Delivery	Problem Solving
Advantages	Multiple locations accessed simultaneously Good accessibility Transportation time and cost reduced Timely	Multiple locations accessed simultaneously Transportation time and cost reduced Minimum training Timely	Large audience potential
Disadvantages	Must be structured Technical difficulties Limited interaction Time and schedule coordination required	May not hold attention Technical difficulties Time and schedule coordination required Audience acceptance limited	May lack specificity Audience acceptance limited
Best Uses	Content delivery Resolving issues Maximizing expertise Over great distances	On-site teaching and training Large groups Localized content	Resolving and clarifying issues Reaching decisions despite distance Task forces Technical groups

Figure 6.7 Features of electronic audio teleconferencing relative to use in an information, educational, or problem-solving learning environment.

ceive large volumes of "perishable" information, and rapidly search through permanent databases. It also has the capability of managing personalized, interactive instructional programs when used in combination with other technologies. Computer-assisted instruc-

Features of Electronic Educational Video	Information Delivery	Education Delivery	Problem Solving
Advantages	Large or small audiences Audience selectable Transportable Recorded on site End product controlled Easily updated Convenient for client Adaptable to locale Timely	Large or small audiences Audience selectable Transportable Recorded on site End product controlled Easily updated High-quality presentations Frees staff from repetition Timely	Large or small audiences Audience selectable Transportable Recorded on site End product controlled Can be interactive High-quality presentations Can have multiple uses
Disadvantages	Training required Audience acceptance required Equipment necessary Advance preparation needed Not generally interactive Competition from commercial programs	Training required Audience acceptance required Equipment necessary Advance preparation needed Expensive Access limited for some states	Training required Audience acceptance required Equipment necessary Advance preparation needed Expensive
Best Uses	Visual topics Timely subjects Simple topics Creating awareness	Motion visuals required	Interaction with computer logic Multiple locations Motion visuals required

Figure 6.8 Features on electronic educational video technology relative to use in an information, educational, or problem-solving learning environment.

Features of Electronic Data Network	Information Delivery	Education Delivery	Problem Solving
Advantages	Information timely Information extensive Information selected by audience	Broad program Audience interactive Self correcting Learning reinforced Educational objectives tested Available anytime	Audience interaction User problem specific Complex problems
Disadvantages	Limited audience size Training needed Technical staff Equipment and network access costly	Limited audience size Equipment and network access costly	Limited audience size Lack of software Subject matter knowledge needed Equipment and network access costly
Best Uses	Database access Electronic mail Timely information delivery	Simulation of complex models Self-paced instruction Complex educational objectives	Support of management decisions

Figure 6.9 Features of electronic data network systems relative to use in an information, educational, or problem-solving learning environment.

tion (CAI), compact disk reader/modem (CD ROM), and interactive video disk kiosk systems are examples of data delivery mechanisms. Provided in Figure 6.9 is an overview of features relating to a data transmission and computer networking system.

ACCESSIBILITY

Garrison (1987) suggests that "the key to appreciating the role and benefit of technology . . . can be found in the issue of access" (p. 42). Inaccessibility becomes more apparent when one considers the two most frequently expressed barriers to participation in adult education—time and place. The challenge becomes one of removing and reducing the barriers while increasing the use of educational technology. Luskin (1980) suggests that if improvements in educational opportunities and access are primary goals of education, then greater use of telecommunications technologies is appropriate and necessary. Delivery systems will need to be designed that will allow learning to become an integral part of the learner's activities in the home and the workplace. Individuals will need to have considerable control over the how, when, and where of the learning.

A number of technologies have been identified which are currently available to enhance the teaching and learning transaction. Questions asked by many practitioners are "Of the technologies that currently exist, what is realistic for my program? What fits my needs?" Limiting factors to consider include availability of funds and funding sources, personnel, and organizational climate. As examples, the factors to be considered in selecting a technology will be examined by reviewing two highly recognized technologies gaining momentum in the adult education field. These are video cassette recorders and the microcomputer. The following discussion provides an overview of the access and availability of these technologies with application to the adult educator.

Video Cassette Recorder

One of the most accessible and affordable educational technologies is the video cassette recorder (VCR). Gueulette (1988) reports that in 1983, *Training Magazine* identified nearly 80 percent of U.S. business and industry as using VCRs for training purposes. Accessibility is enhanced since national network and public broadcast television can be recorded for use at a later date to enhance learning at the "teachable moment." Also, university and public libraries stock a variety of instructional materials on one-half inch video cassette tape, making it easily accessible through the local community library or via interlibrary loan. The key to the successful use of educational video is planning. Suggested steps in the planning process include:

1. Identifying the appropriate level of instruction

2. Preparing the student for the delivery mode

3. Coordinating the follow-up discussion to the video presentation

4. Providing support services by the university for video-based instruction

An important advantage of the VCR is that instructional material can be viewed in the learner's home at whatever time is convenient and at the student's own pace. And, the videotape can be viewed repeatedly, paused, or replayed at any time by the learner, allowing for the inclusion of interactivity based on the program design (e.g., inclusion of print-base programmed instruction, audiotape, and problem solving in conjunction with the videotape).

Gueulette (1988) suggests that the most effective use of educational video is found in the following:

1. Introduction of new materials or ideas

2. Review of previously learned material

3. Visual support of ideas or concepts

4. Clarification of special points

5. Reinforcement of key concepts

Adult students appear to work most efficiently when they are given a framework in which to learn. However, adults also like to be creative within the framework and "modify" their learning to suit their own needs and preferences. The use of educational video is conducive to this notion. Guidelines for using the delivery mode include:

1. When planning the course outline/content, all instructional resources should be listed, including educational video(s).

2. On the day the educational video is to be used, prepare the student as best possible. Remind the student that taking notes dur-

ing a video presentation can be distracting and nonproductive due to a process called transmediation. This is a change that occurs when information is transferred from one medium to another, implying that something is lost or changed in the process.

3. Inform the learners that a discussion will follow the visual presentation so they can feel less anxious about "getting it." This allows for understanding to formulate when the discussion is added to the visual presentation.

In order to solidify the information given in the video presentation, answer questions, or correct any misunderstandings, a discussion following the videotape and facilitated by the instructor is helpful. The discussion should include:

1. Guided questioning of the information.

2. Integration of the visual information into the regular classroom presentation. (The inclusion of some of the new information given in the visual on a quiz or test adds value to the visual, justifies its use, and promotes motivation in the students.)

3. Student/teacher discussion regarding the appropriateness and usefulness of the visual or other technology itself.

The fourth step previously mentioned in the planning of educational video involved the provision of university support services. Gunawardena (1989) suggests four areas in which support needs to be provided, including: a) study skills, b) faculty accessibility, c) feedback, and d) library access.

Microcomputer Technology

Another very popular, accessible, and affordable type of educational technology both in and out of the classroom is the microcomputer. The use of computers has progressed, especially in the area of enhancing interactivity in learning. New coursework being devised with touchscreen capability and the maneuverable mouse has been helpful to many students, especially those without access to libraries or schools. The assistance of computers in the area of interactive video has also allowed the learner a wide range of interactivity, beginning with a basic level of question/answer and moving toward a higher, more complex level such as simulation, in which problem solving becomes the critical factor. And, computers are being used more and more for facilitating basic skills to adults. Lewis (1988) found in a study of 666 adult basic education students that in general the students are both interested in and comfortable with computers. She also found that older women who have been away from school for a long time are the least confident about their ability to use computers. The recommendations by Lewis (1988) are relevant for adult learners in general. She suggests the following teaching techniques to enhance a computer learning experience:

1. Demystify the computer.

2. Attempt to ascertain the learners' worst fears.

3. Start with the basics.

4. Recount your own personal experiences as a beginning computer user.

5. Avoid jargon or buzz words.

6. Take things slowly.

7. Don't give students too much information at once.

8. Remind learners that they do not have to memorize everything.

9. Provide numerous and frequent opportunities for hands-on experience.

10. Promote learning partnerships.

11. Utilize learners as peer tutors to assist others.

12. Encourage group work.

13. Encourage learners to share their successes as well as their problems.

14. Reassure users that it is all right to make mistakes.

15. Reserve time for open discussion.

16. Whenever possible, hold computer courses in neutral or nontraditional locations such as lounges or libraries.

17. Invite women to be guest speakers.

DISTANT DELIVERY SYSTEMS

A distinguishing feature of the concept of distance education is that it is a means of extending access to education to those learners who might otherwise be excluded. Garrison and Shale (1987) suggest three essential criteria in characterizing distance education relative to educational technology:

1. The majority of educational communication between (among) teacher and student(s) occurs noncontiguously.

2. Two-way communication is required between (among) teacher and student(s) for the purpose of facilitating and supporting the educational process.

3. Technology is used to mediate the necessary two-way communication.

Distance education is unquestionably linked to the technology of delivery. However, technology must be seen in light of an educational perspective with the essential characteristics capable of providing access and support to the learners identified. Many of the educational technologies currently in use are implemented in the area of distance education as well as in the formal institutional setting. However, both cost and equipment requirements escalate considerably with such implementation. Often, it is only those states or systems with substantial funding sources, resources, and student numbers that can employ full-scale educational technology for the distant learner. Ironically, those states that are the most in need, such as geographically large western states with sparse populations, are often the ones that do not have the population base to justify even a moderately sophisticated distance education system. However, one western state, with the assistance of a major grant, was able to implement a practical distance education system which included slow-scan TV, electronic blackboards, two-way audio, and a fax machine supported by print-base instructional materials.

Satellite programming has been of interest to a variety of institutions and educational service providers involved in the concept of distance education. However, the use of satellite downlink capability requires an appropriate satellite dish and a substantial reception fee. Thus, the equipment and fees require a fairly large learner audience to result in a cost-effective educational broadcast. Even a technology as simple as audio teleconferencing requires special telephone wiring and bridges. In addition, the quality of transmission is sometimes quite poor and may hinder the most enthusiastic learner.

Regardless of the choice of educational technology for the delivery of distance education, the following suggestions are offered to preserve and enrich the teaching and learning transaction.

1. The instructors should be selected by their classroom styles, their willingness to adapt to the medium, and their support of and belief in the system. Often, what works in a "live" classroom will also work with video.

2. A facilitator should be present at each remote site to maintain equipment and answer questions.

3. The instructor should prepare a facilitator guide as well as student materials so that the facilitator is knowledgeable of the overall plan.

In addition, Norton (1985) suggests that adult educators must take into consideration a variety of factors in selecting and implementing educational technology before the actual teaching begins. These include the following.

1. As the electronic technologies become the defining technologies, educators must gain an understanding of the history of technology, the role of technology in change, the social and psychological impacts of technology, and the implications of current changes for education.

2. Adult educators must devise new definitions of classroom learning in addition to finding a new understanding of the learning environment.

3. Educators of adults must consider alternatives to the traditional curriculum and devise new instructional strategies involving educational technologies.

4. Adult educators must not only know about the electronic technologies, but must also learn how to develop and select software for use with the computer that facilitates learning.

As Gunawardena (1988, p. 174) reported, "the technologies are far less troublesome than the intra-institutional, political and bureaucratic integration of the program." The larger the system, the more complex the problems. The recommendation is to concentrate on the planning, preparation, and student interaction with the educational opportunity.

SUMMARY

Electronic media journals are replete with information regarding new technologies. Amazing feats with compact video disks that read from memory (CD ROM) and interactive digital video (DVI) are impressive. New work with holographic images is inspiring. However, it is beyond the scope of this chapter to predict the future of the rapidly changing technology arena. The three purposes identified as central to this chapter were (1) to provide a discussion on how technology can be used to enhance the teaching and learning transaction, (2) to graphically display the usefulness of technology in a variety of learning environments, and (3) to provide criteria with which instructors can select appropriate technology based on type, accessibility, and effectiveness. It was also suggested that educational technologies can enhance the teaching and learning transaction in many areas. Three of the most important include the teaching of life tasks that require knowledge, skills, and attitudes, in addition to accommodating for a variety of adult learning styles, and at the same time allowing the student optimal control over content, structure, and evaluation of the learning.

Several educational uses of technology (i.e., information delivery, education delivery, and problem solving) were discussed with figures providing an emphasis on the advantages and disadvantages of selected technologies. The figures were designed to help the practitioner select the level and type of educational technology for a specific need. Finally, some of the underutilized, but highly accessible educational technology was described. Specific attention was directed toward the use of educational video and the potential for educational computer programs as a basis for interactive learning.

Current trends suggest that perhaps the future of educational technology is more a change in perspective than a change in hardware. In many instances, the educator's mode of thinking about the usefulness of a particular technology has not yet caught up with the development of the technology. Just as frontiersmen could not foresee the long-range impact of the telephone, we are still myopic regarding the usefulness of most educational technology.

Educators have applied the principles of andragogy to technological innovations and recognize its usefulness, for example, in self-directed projects, application learning, and for distant delivery. However, due to a lack of experience with educational technology, adult educators may feel uncomfortable using these media in the classroom and demonstrate a less than assertive approach in the teaching and learning transaction.

As the discipline of adult education directs its attention toward the twenty-first century, specific areas relevant to educational technology, involving selection, implementation, and management, will need to be addressed. These areas include:

1. Exploring new ways of thinking about the use of technology in adult education with the emphasis on the teaching and learning transaction rather than on the latest technological device.

2. Purchasing basic, but high quality and versatile equipment/hardware, and being imaginative in its use.

3. Purchasing high quality and appropriate software.

4. Excluding technology unless it will enhance the learning experience. Adults do not tolerate "irrelevant" learning no matter how sophisticated the equipment.

5. Developing an educational technology philosophy to provide a basis for making decisions on the use or selection of technology.

6. Building in evaluative mechanisms for determining the effectiveness of implementation to the learner, the teacher, and the institution.

It has been suggested that in the future it will be the variety of provision and the quality of interaction with the teacher and learning materials that will attract and sustain the adult learner. Delivery systems will be required to integrate learning into the life of the adult with a minimum of disruption and inconvenience. To do this, effective communication systems will be necessary.

Garrison (1987) suggests that of any educational sector, continuing education for adults will see the greatest growth and change during the 1990s. The role of educational technology will greatly influence all aspects of this change. Students will be expecting and demanding greater use of educational technology which in turn will provide equity of access and ongoing support and interaction during the learning process. The challenge for the educator is to integrate the new technologies into a functional delivery system that is open to all adult learners.

REFERENCES

Bradford, L. (1958). The teaching-learning transaction. *Adult Education, 8*(3), 135–145.

Burnham, B., & Seamons, R. (1987). Exploring the landscape of electronic distance education. *Lifelong Learning: An Omnibus of Practice and Research, 11*(2), 8–11.

Electronic Technology Task Force Report. (1985). *Electronic technology: Impact on extension delivery systems* (Task Force Report). University Park: The Pennsylvania State University, Northeast Computer Institute.

Ely, D. (Ed.). (1988). *Educational media and technology yearbook: 1988.* Englewood, CO.: Libraries Unlimited.

Gagné, R. (1977). *The conditions of learning* (3rd ed.). New York: Holt, Rinehart, and Winston.

Gagné, R. (1985). *The conditions of learning* (4th ed.). New York: Holt, Rinehart, and Winston.

Gagné, R., & L. Briggs. (1974). *Principles of instructional design.* New York: Holt, Rinehart, and Winston.

Garrison, R. (1987). The role of technology in continuing education. In R. G. Brockett (Ed.), *Continuing education in the year 2000* (pp. 41–53). New Directions for Continuing Education, no. 36. San Francisco: Jossey-Bass.

Garrison, R., & Shale, D. (1987). Mapping the boundaries of distance education: Problems in defining the field. *American Journal of Distance Education, 1*(1), 7–13.

Gueulette, D. (1988). Better ways to use television for adult learning. *Lifelong Learning: An Omnibus of Practice and Research, 11*(6), 22–25.

Gunawardena, C. (1988). Current approaches to using communications technologies for delivering adult continuing/professional education. *Proceedings of the 30th Annual Adult Education Research
Conference* (pp. 171–176). Madison: University of Wisconsin-
Madison.

Heaney, T. (1976). Interactive media: An application of media as
process. *Community College Education, 7,* 42–45.

Kester, B., & Gueulette, D. (1981). Interactive media for adult
learning. *Media and Adult Learning, 4*(1), 17–20.

Knowles, M. (1983). How the media can make it or bust it in
education. *Media and Adult Learning, 5*(2), 3–4.

Lewis, L. (1988). Adults and computer anxiety: Fact or fiction?
Lifelong Learning: An Omnibus of Practice and Research, 11(8),
5–8.

Luskin, B. (1980). Telecommunications: A prism of access for adult
learning. *T.H.E. Journal, 7*(5), 43–50.

Meierhenry, W. (1981). Adult education and media and technology.
Media and Technology in Adult Learning, 11(1), 3–8.

Norton, P. (1985). An agenda for technology and education: Eight
imperatives. *Educational Technology, 25*(1), 15–20.

Pratt, D. (1987). Technology and instructional functions. In J.A.
Niemi & D.D. Gooler (Eds.), *Technologies for learning outside
the classroom* (pp. 73–87). New Directions for Continuing Education, no. 34. San Francisco: Jossey-Bass.

Schwen, T. (1977). Professional scholarship in educational technology: Criteria for inquiry. *AV Communication Review, 25,* 35–79.

Travers, R. (1982). *Essential of learning: The new cognitive learning for students of education.* New York: MacMillan.

CHAPTER 7

Evaluating the Teaching and Learning Process

PAULETTE T. BEATTY
LINDA L. BENEFIELD
LANI J. LINHART

To adult education professionals, the idea of evaluation is not new. We have experienced it in many shapes and sizes. The way in which we choose to define evaluation has, typically, very much to do with the various purposes which evaluation might serve and the various stakeholders in the educational process. Frequently, evaluation is associated with comprehensive program review in order to meet basic accountability requirements of funding or sponsoring agencies (Brinkerhoff, 1987; Deshler, 1984; French-Lazovik; 1982; Herman, 1989). Periodically, annual performance appraisals of instructional staff are conducted by administrative personnel for purposes of continuation, termination, or salary decisions. Yet, at other times, evaluation is conducted in response to legislative mandate such as when major infusion of public money is involved. Community leadership may also be a significant consitutency which demands a review of ongoing programs designed specifically to meet indigenous needs. The courts too may have a vested interest in the evaluation of programs since failure to train is an issue which may be brought to court as liability suits are reviewed.

The intent of our efforts in this chapter is not to ignore these purposes and the array of important stakeholders in the educational enterprise, but rather to emphasize the facilitator and the learner as the most directly impacted and the central stakeholders in the teaching and learning transaction. Our central focus in evaluating the teaching and learning transaction is to maximize learning for all participants, both learners and facilitators of learning.

Six closely associated purposes for evaluating instruction have been identified which also merit our attention. They are:

1. To improve the instruction

2. To promote individual growth and self-evaluation

3. To assess the degree of demonstrable attainment by the teacher

4. To diagnose future learning needs

5. To enhance one's own sense of merit or worth

6. To identify and/or clarify desired behaviors (Seaman & Fellenz, 1989)

Our working definition, which would well serve our central and associated purposes, is that evaluation is the mutual, interactive, and systematic process of identifying, gathering, and analyzing information in order to make decisions which would enhance learning for all persons involved.

In this chapter we first present a framework which we developed to guide us in our thinking about the evaluation of instruction from the mutual perspective of the facilitator and the learner. Within this framework are identified the most central issues in the evaluation process. Second, we expand upon the framework and provide a set of practical strategies which could be employed in focusing upon the central evaluation issues to be addressed. This section also provides the criteria which guided us in our selection of the specific strategies. Last, we offer guidelines for designing an evaluation plan.

EVALUATION FRAMEWORK

The evaluation process, as we envision it, involves focusing upon issues which are paramount at the initiation of the learning experience, during the transactions of the learning experience, and in the final phases of the learning experience when outgrowth issues are central. Therefore, the evaluation framework is designed to help the professional focus upon three central questions: Who are we? What are we doing together? How has it affected us?

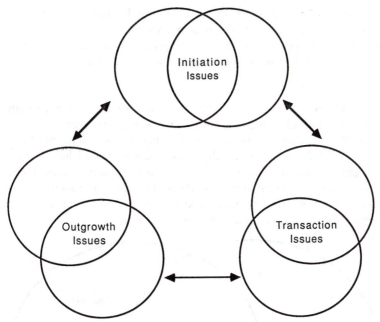

Figure 7.1 A framework for evaluating the teaching and learning process.

Figure 7.1 is a depiction of the framework for the evaluation process. Each individual circle represents the facilitator or learner. The intersecting circles represent the meshing of each issue and signify the importance of adult learners being involved in every aspect of the learning experience (Rosenblum, 1985). The initiation issues can be one and the same, in certain areas, for both facilitator and learner. For example, both facilitator and learner come to the learning situation with prior life experiences which influence their thoughts and feelings. Transaction issues are also shared by facilitator and learner. For example, concentration is impaired for everyone when the facilities are inadequate: poor lighting, uncomfortable seating, and room temperatures which are too hot or too cold. Finally, outgrowth issues can cover common areas of concern for facilitator and learner, such as when each assesses the gains made during the learning situation. The initiation issues and the outgrowth issues are linked together as before and after phases since these are parallel in many aspects. In the framework the transaction issues have a separately defined purpose; however, unlike the initiation and outgrowth issues, they are continually occuring as interactions to be assessed. The evaluation cycle is, consequently, a flowing, continual process in which the issues may relate to each other at various times during the teaching and learning process.

Initiation Issues

When focusing upon initiation issues, we are concerned with what the individual learner and teacher bring to the learning situation. Part of what distinguishes the practice of adult education from teaching children is that as adults age and mature they have both a greater amount of, and more differentiated, life experiences. Thus, issues that are present at the initiation of the current learning situation will impact the instructor and learners as individuals and as a group. Figure 7.2 presents these initiation issues.

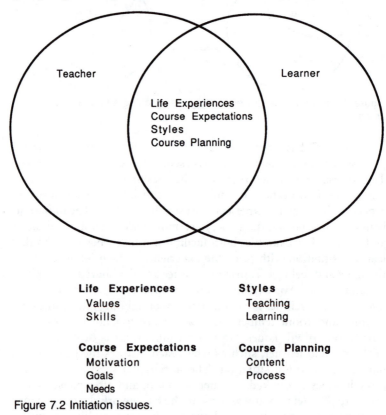

Life Experiences
Values
Skills

Styles
Teaching
Learning

Course Expectations
Motivation
Goals
Needs

Course Planning
Content
Process

Figure 7.2 Initiation issues.

We look at initiation issues from four perspectives: life experiences, course expectations, learning and teaching styles, and course planning. By life experiences we mean the values and skills that both the adult learner and facilitator bring to the learning situation. Course expectations include the goals each individual may have for the learning situation, the motivation each may have in participating, and the needs each would express regarding what she or he would like to gain from the learning experience. In discussing teaching and learning styles we focus upon what an instructor actually does when teaching and facilitating, and what style is most comfortable and effective for a learner when faced with acquiring new information. Course planning encompasses the processes to be employed and the content or topics to be covered in the learning situation. We see these as most amenable to a transactional process with the adult learner having a fully participatory role in the planning.

Transaction Issues

Transaction issues are at the heart of the learning process and not enough can be said about the need for assessing their impact. Figure 7.3 presents the transaction issues. Certainly the idea of formative evaluation is a key concept in our thinking about transaction issues. We have included four areas that are particularly important: course content, course methods, interpersonal process, and learning climate.

In viewing course content as an evaluation issue, the learner and instructor satisfaction levels should be assessed to determine the impact of the content upon them. Meaningfulness is of particular importance to adults as they come to the learning situation with current needs and problems they wish to see addressed. Linking the content of the learning experience to satisfaction level is therefore crucial. Course methods encompass the actual processes employed by the instructor to facilitate learning. Determining effectiveness of methods and learner as well as teacher satisfaction with the learning experience is essential in assessing meaningfulness. Interpersonal process takes the total group interaction into consideration. Evaluation of how the learners are interacting as a group is important as each participant represents a rich resource in the learning process of his or her colleagues. Consequently, the transactional process in learning is emphasized. Finally, under the category of transaction issues, the total learning climate is considered. This includes both

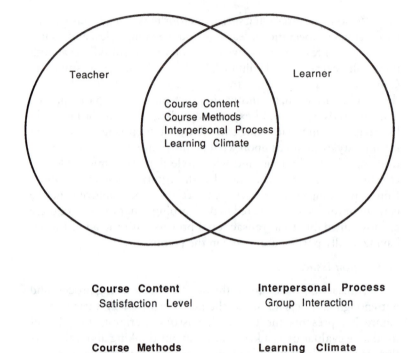

Course Content	Interpersonal Process
Satisfaction Level	Group Interaction

Course Methods	Learning Climate
Individualized	Emotional
Small Group	Physical
Large Group	

Figure 7.3 Transaction issues

the emotional and physical facets of the learning situation. In acquiring new learning old learning can be challenged. A level of trust needs to develop so learners can feel free to question personal bits of old learning with the least amount of threat. In addition, the adult's physical comfort needs to be addressed so as not to interfere with learning.

Outgrowth Issues

Perhaps we could say that outgrowth issues are what are traditionally thought of as evaluation issues. Was the learning experience successful? Would we do it again? What would we change if we were to do it again?

We see these issues as inextricably linked to the initiation

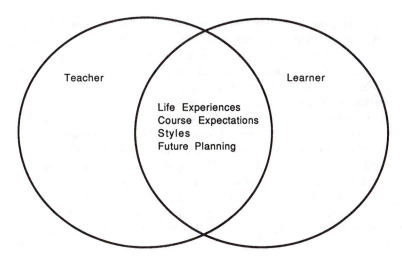

Life Experiences
Personal/Professional Enrichment
Interpersonal Skills Development
Unanticipated Learning

Course Expectations
Goals Met
Needs Met

Styles
Teaching Adaptation
Learning Flexibility

Future Planning
Teacher
Learner

Figure 7.4 Outgrowth issues

issues. The only way of assessing if we have gained from the learning experience is to know what we came with and what we wanted to achieve. There will be direct parallels between initiation issues and outgrowth issues. Figure 7.4 presents the outgrowth issues.

Life experiences are dealt with, this time, from three perspectives: the learner's personal and professional enrichment, the level of skill gained in interpersonal/group interaction, and the unanticipated learning that has resulted through the learning experience that has taken place. In discussing course expectations we evaluate whether an acceptable level of satisfaction was achieved by the individual adult learners, whether goals and needs were met, and what the learning outcomes were in terms of actually gaining new information or skills. An evaluation of learning and teaching styles, as an outgrowth issue, focuses upon the degree to which the facilitator and the learners were able to make accommodations in style and develop a broader repertoire of teaching and/or learning skills. Thus, learners should be able to assess how their own learning styles aided or impaired them and what appropriate modifications could be made for future learning experiences. In addition, the instructor needs to reflect upon his or her teaching style and the degree to which it aided or impaired the learning experience. Lastly, the initiation issue of course planning parallels the outgrowth issue of future planning. One dimension of future planning is that both the learner and facilitator are able to verbalize the impact of the learning experience upon their futures and are able to capitalize upon this experience. Ideally, an evaluation of the learning situation's impact on future planning would yield information on how well the learning succeeded as well as its impact upon each adult's life.

EVALUATION STRATEGIES

We have selected twelve specific strategies which we feel can be used to assess these evaluation issues. Each strategy is linked to one of the evaluation issues identified. Table 7.1 shows the relationship of strategies to evaluation issues. Of course, these are not the only strategies possible. We have given suggestions for others that might be used and hope that readers will also make up their own.

Five criteria were used for selecting which strategies to present and which to focus on for each evaluation issue. We believe that each strategy should be:

1. Interactive—engaging all participants actively

2. Egalitarian—fostering a mutual partnership in the learning situation between learner and facilitator

3. Relevant—applying broadly to a wide variety of groups

4. Efficient—making few demands on the instructional budget and requiring no more than a maximum of one hour to complete

5. Flexible—adapting to a wide variety of situations

Table 7.1
Evaluation Strategies

Initiations Issues	Strategies
Life Experiences	Peer Interview
Learning Styles	Discussion Groups
Course Expectations	Brainstorming
Course Planning	Nominal Group Technique
Transaction Issues	
Course Content	Investigative Reporting
Course Methods	Quality Circles
Interpersonal Processes	Participant Observation
Learning Climate	Problem-Solving Groups
Outgrowth Issues	
Life Experiences	Buzz Groups
Learning Styles	Debate Teams
Course Expectations	Creative Activity
Future Planning	Panel/Role Play

Strategies for Initiation Issues

Life Experiences: Peer Interview. Adults come to a new learning situation with a sense of themselves which has been shaped by their cumulative life experiences. These include self-concepts and self-esteem, past successes and failures as learners, attitudes and values, potential assets and possible liabilities, and directly or indirectly related experiences and skills. Ingalls (1973) has shown a sensitivity to the needs and interests of adults in his trainer's guide. Brundage and Mackeracher (1980) and Smith (1982) are also useful resources when thinking about characteristics of adults and the variety of life experiences they bring to the learning situation.

In deciding on an evaluation strategy that would address life experience issues and promote the transactional process, we felt that peer interviews could best capture the richness of what each learner would choose to share about himself or herself. A key element in the peer interview is atmosphere. A relaxed, informal atmosphere is highly desirable to encourage free-flowing conversation. Therefore, whenever possible, make arrangements for a comfortable physical environment. Some suggestions might include: providing some simple refreshments; arranging the room informally with low lighting, background music, and comfortable seating; or having the participants adjourn to a lounge or coffee shop when conducting the interviews.

The following steps should be employed in conducting the peer interview strategy:

1. Provide all participants with a 3 × 5 index card on which to record biographical information such as: name, address, day and/or evening phone numbers, type of employment (if applicable), and any other information which would be important. This will subsequently be shared with the peer interviewer and included on a roster for distribution to all participants. (5 minutes)

2. Arbitrarily divide the group into dyads. Give each participant a copy of the interview guidelines. This could be a preprinted sheet of paper outlining specific topics to be covered in the interview. Provide enough room for taking notes during the interview. Possible topics could include the following:

   —Personal Information: Who are you?

   —Career Information: What are your greatest challenges? What are your greatest accomplishments? What are your future plans?

   —Learning Experiences: What are the most important new things you have learned, either formally or informally, over the past two years?

   —Leisure Time Activities: What do you like to do on your time off? What skills do you need to engage in this activity?

   —Just For Fun: What animal, bird, fish, or whatever best describes your personality?

   (5 minutes)

3. Instruct each dyad to take 10 minutes apiece to interview their partner, focusing upon information contained on the biographical data card and answering questions posed in the interview guidelines. Advise participants that peer interviewers will share this information with the entire group. The instructor needs to remain as unobtrusive as possible. (25 minutes)

4. Reconvene the group. Have each interviewer introduce to the rest of the group the person he or she interviewed, taking 3 to 5 minutes each. The instructor may set the stage and begin this process by sharing the same personal information. (25 minutes)

5. Collect biographical data cards and completed interview guides for subsequent development of class roster and instructor use. (5 minutes)

Learning Styles: Discussion Groups. The initiation issue to be served through this evaluation strategy is learning styles. Both learning and teaching styles should be issues of concern in the transactional learning process. The approaches one selects for instruction or learning are frequently dictated by one's particular style. Not all approaches are equally suited for all participants. Consequently, satisfaction with and ultimate benefit from the learning experience are impacted.

Although the concept of learning style has not been adequately researched, there remains an "intuitive appeal" for its use as a teaching aid. Adult educators need to become increasingly sensitive to the different learning styles adults bring with them into the learning experience. Bonham (1988) offers suggestions on how an adult educator might best utilize various learning style instruments.

Various instruments are available for measuring learning and/or cognitive style: the *Canfield Learning Styles Inventory* (1983), the *Kolb Learning Style Inventory* (1976), and the *Schmeck and Ribich Inventory and Learning Processes* (1977, 1978) to name a few.

We have chosen the *Group Embedded Figures Test* (GEFT) which was designed to measure field dependence/independence (Oltman, Raskin, & Witkin, 1971). It is a timed, self-scored paper and pencil test that is intended to be administered in a group setting. The object of the test is to find the simple form in the more complex design and trace it with a pencil.

The field dependence/independence cognitive style and its impact on education and learning have been studied. Briefly, persons who are field independent impose structure and organization upon situations, focus upon detail and specifics, and perceive themselves as more independent. They have an easier time solving problems and learning material that is relatively abstract and unstructured.

Field independent persons may be easily overloaded when the facilitator presents a great deal of organizational stimuli since they are already imposing their own organization. Field dependent persons, by contrast, view things more globally, are sensitive to surrounding stimuli, and perceive themselves as more social. They are more negatively affected by criticism and more likely to respond with greater motivation when rewarded and/or praised. The facilitator may need to provide greater organizational stimuli for field dependent persons as an aid in structuring learning. Witkin (1976) and Witkin, Moore, Goodenough, and Cox (1977) are just two sources for detailed explanations of these cognitive styles.

Thus, knowing a learner's preferred style can be helpful in the learning situation. It can guide the instructor in presenting material and in pinpointing why a particular learner may be having difficulty. In addition, having the instructor aware of his or her preferred learning style is equally beneficial. There is evidence that instructors prefer certain teaching methods based on field independence or dependence characteristics. For example, field dependent instructors are more comfortable with group discussion techniques, whereas field independent instructors prefer lecture style or discovery learning techniques.

The following steps should be employed in conducting the discussion group strategy:

1. Distribute the test booklet to each participant and walk through the instructions and examples with them. (5 minutes)

2. Administer the test according to the published instructions and guide the participants in scoring their tests. (20 minutes)

3. List scores on the board along a continuum with the highest field dependent scores on one end and the highest field independent scores on the other end. Lead the group in a brief discussion regarding the characteristics of each style of learning. Be sure to emphasize that there are no right or wrong learning styles, just differences. (10 minutes)

4. Divide the group into teams of four or five persons each. Group those with similar learning styles together. Have each team appoint a recorder. Provide newsprint, markers, and masking tape for each team. Instruct each team to discuss and

list strategies they have used in the past to help them in learning new information. Have each team recorder post the list. (15 minutes)

5. The facilitator should lead a group discussion comparing and contrasting the strategies used by field dependent versus field independent persons. Include in the discussion how persons with one preferred style might learn strategies from the other to cope with various learning situations. (10 minutes)

Course Expectations: Brainstorming. We viewed the evaluation issues attached to course expectations as including goals, motivations, and needs. In the transactional learning process these are shared between instructor and learner. The learners will have expectations for learning experiences which are quite specific in nature. These, once shared, can be capitalized upon by the instructor to enhance the learning experience.

There are several possibilities for tapping into the interactive aspect of course expectations. Darkenwald and Valentine (1986) have developed the *Adult Classroom Environment Scale* which could be used to elicit expectations about classroom social environment. Eitington (1984) offers a number of activities to assist in focusing on course expectations.

We have chosen to look at the instrument designed by Pratt (1979): The *Instructional Process/Environment Questionnaire* (IPEQ). Pratt developed his assessment instrument specifically to use with adult learners in a wide variety of adult educational settings. Sixteen components were included which clustered into five distinct groups. "Developing an Adult-to-Adult Working Relationship" includes clarifying purpose, making a demand for work, accepting individual differences, sharing feelings, and developing trust. "Developing Mutual Understanding, Support, and Responsibility" includes establishing goals and content of instruction, sharing responsibility and authority, developing trust, and using positive reinforcement. "Dealing with Closure and Ending" includes allowing for practice or application of learning, synthesizing content, and dealing with the culmination of the group membership experience. "Establishing Role Clarity and Credibility" includes explaining roles and responsibilities, developing trust, establishing content credibility, and recognizing and using the diversity of adult groups. "Guarding the Contract" includes holding to focus and sharing feelings.

The instrument is designed to be given either before the learning experience when participants are asked what they would prefer in the learning situation or at the conclusion of the learning experience when participants are asked what they actually experienced. We have chosen to emphasize the learner's preferences before the learning experience. In order to tap into the adult learner's personal expectations regarding the learning experience we have chosen the technique of brainstorming which can be effectively linked with the completion of the Pratt instrument. Brainstorming is a well-known and popular procedure introduced in the 1950s. Forsyth (1983), Johnson and Johnson (1987), and Eitington (1984) offer excellent descriptions of the technique.

The following steps should be employed in conducting the brainstorming strategy:

1. Administer the IPEQ in a class session following the instructions provided with the instrument. (15 minutes)

2. Have participants score their questionnaires. Average the group result for each factor measured. Present these group means for each factor on the blackboard. (15 minutes)

3. Have the group divide into teams of five or six members to begin brainstorming. Use the results of the IPEQ as the basis for the session. Each group is to suggest specific actions that the instructor could take to produce the most positive psychological climate for learning. Have each group select a recorder. Provide the recorder with newsprint, a marker, and masking tape so that ideas generated may be written down and posted. Hand each member a preprinted list of the following brainstorming rules:

   —Express freely any idea that comes to mind no matter how unique or unusual.

   —Do not evaluate any of the ideas in any way.

   —Generate as many ideas as possible.

   —Modify and extend each other's ideas.

   (15 minutes)

4. Have each team choose a spokesperson to share the results of the brainstorming session with the entire group. (10 minutes)

5. The facilitator will summarize the discussion and indicate attempts that will be made to accommodate the suggestions, needs, and expectations expressed. (5 minutes)

Course Planning: Nominal Group Technique. The content of a particular educational experience is a primary responsibility of the instructor. We, as adult educators, however, feel that adults as learners have a great deal to offer the planning process. Furthermore, participation in planning the learning experience leads to enhanced motivation on the part of the learner.

The nominal group technique promotes group interaction as well as individual participation in the group process for generating ideas about a specific topic. It is also helpful in eliciting a greater number of ideas, in leaving participants more satisfied with the final decision, and in avoiding conflict over issues that could generate emotional reactions. We have chosen this as a valuable tool for gathering input from individual learners regarding course planning. It also is valuable in promoting the transactional process. Forsyth (1983) and Eitington (1984) are two sources for a more complete outline of this technique.

The following steps should be employed in conducting the nominal group technique strategy:

1. The instructor writes on a blackboard or flip chart the issue to be discussed, stated simply and clearly. One example of an issue is "Topics to be Covered." Be sure each participant understands the issue. The instructor will provide a skeleton framework of the broad areas that will be addressed in the course, including a few examples of topics that might be covered. (10 minutes)

2. Have each participant silently write down ideas for topics that would address the course content. (10 minutes)

3. Each participant, in turn, states one idea with the instructor listing it on the blackboard. This sharing continues around the group until all ideas have been listed. (15 minutes)

4. The group will discuss each item. It is important that the discussion focuses primarily on clarification of the ideas, not on qualitative remarks. (15 minutes)

5. Pass out index cards to each participant. Ask that they indicate on the card, in order of preference, their top five choices from those listed on the blackboard. (5 minutes)

6. The instructor collects the cards and averages the rankings to yield a group decision. The participants are then informed of the decision. (5 minutes)

Strategies for Transaction Issues

Course Content: Investigative Reporting. Ensuring learner satisfaction with course content is a continual challenge faced by the adult educator. As the content of what is to be learned in an educational program is addressed, many demands will be placed upon the learner. One of the greatest safeguards for ensuring that the demands of learning are met is to secure a high level of intrinsic motivation. Motivation is enhanced when the content of the course is meaningful to the learner. For most learning experiences, meaningfulness is achieved when the learning is perceived as relevant and when it can be applied in the real world of the learner. We have chosen to look at the challenge of ensuring learning application or transfer even though this is not the only question which could be posed when considering the issue of course content. Eitington (1984) presents many activities for overcoming the problem of the transfer of learning. Some of these activities can be employed in evaluating the degree to which transfer of learning is actually occurring.

We have chosen investigative reporting as the strategy for evaluating satisfaction and applicability of course content. This strategy is most effectively employed at the conclusion of a given segment of a course. The investigative reporters' function is twofold. First, they must probe in gathering critical information from the informant. Second, they must present, in a cogent and unified fashion, the information gathered. This sets the stage for subsequent decision making. In information gathering, they typically utilize a journalist's six questions: who, what, when, where, why, and how. In information reporting, they typically utilize a public forum, such as a press conference, a written brief, or an editorial.

The following steps should be employed in conducting the investigative reporting strategy:

1. After the completion of a specific segment of a course, divide the participants of the program into small groups of four persons each. The facilitator distributes to all participants a listing of key ideas or concepts covered in that segment of the course. Have the groups decide which one of their members will play the role of the investigative reporter. The facilitator provides each investigative reporter with three copies of a preprinted sheet on which to record the report. Each sheet contains the following questions:

   —Who is applying the key idea?

   —What key idea is being applied?

   —When is it able to be applied?

   —Where is it applied?

   —Why is it being applied?

   —How is it being applied?

   —What is the key idea that is most difficult to apply?

   —Why is it so difficult to apply?

   —What could make it easier?

   (5 minutes)

2. The investigative reporter begins the questioning process, spending 5 minutes with each participant, focusing upon the first six questions. Investigative reporters make notes on the form provided. While one member is being interviewed, other members may observe, but should not intrude. (15 minutes)

3. The investigative reporter continues questioning by posing the final three questions on the investigative reporting form relating to difficulties in applying key ideas. (15 minutes)

4. At the completion of the final question, the investigative reporters should be grouped together in a fishbowl fashion with the participants sitting on the outer circle. The facilitator provides the investigators with a preprinted transparency which is divided into three columns. The first column is a listing of the key concepts; the second and third columns are tallies. The second

column is labeled "easy to transfer/apply" and the third column is labeled "difficult to transfer/apply." The investigative reporters then tally the group's responses to the key concepts on the transparency. (10 minutes)

5. The facilitator then leads the group in a discussion of all of the questions covered by the investigators. Discussion should include reasons for the ease of transferability of some key concepts and suggestions for improving the transferability of others. (15 minutes)

Course Methods: Quality Circles. Methods for facilitating learning vary tremendously. The decision to select any given method for facilitating learning is routinely made after considering four major factors: the needs and preferences of the learner; the skills and preferences of the facilitator; the nature of the content and the related purposes for the educational program; and an array of contextual realities. These realities include the expectations and concerns of institutional sponsors, the availability of additional leadership personnel, the allocation of time available for a learning activity, and accessibility to material resources such as suitable facilities, money, and equipment. The learner, the facilitator, the content, and the context are all critical considerations. The evaluation of any method employed for instruction cannot ignore the influence which these considerations must and should play.

Bergevin, Morris, and Smith (1963) provide an excellent resource for evaluating course processes; evaluative criteria are provided for each method or technique addressed. In addition, Eitington (1984) has a number of procedures for evaluating instructional methods.

We have chosen to employ a quality circle approach to the evaluation of the methods of instruction. In business and industry, quality circles are used as an approach to participative management. Casner-Lotto & Associates (1988) provide an overview of participatory management techniques in the use of training strategies. Quality circles consist of approximately six to eight employees who volunteer to study a particular situation or problem in their work environment and offer recommendations for implementing change to management. In the context of adult education, quality circles consist of participants who would study a particular facet of the educational program and subsequently offer guidance for the facilitator.

The following steps should be employed in conducting the quality circles strategy:

1. At the beginning of a segment of a learning experience, the facilitator should obtain volunteers to constitute quality circles of six to eight members each. The facilitator will develop a two part, open-ended questionnaire for each quality circle to use as a basis for gathering information and for making recommendations to the instructor. The first part will deal with suggestions for instructor contribution; the second part will deal with participant contribution. All participants should be instructed to record personal observations and impressions on the questionnaire during the progression of the course segment. The questionnaire should include the following:

   —What could the instructor have done to have made this segment more effective?

   —What did the instructor do that was helpful to learning?

   —What did the instructor do that was not helpful to learning?

   —What changes does the instructor need to make to facilitate learning?

   —What could I, the participant, have done personally to have made this segment more effective for my own learning?

   —What could I have done to make this segment more effective for other members' learning?

   —What will I do in the future to maximize my own learning?

   —What will I do in the future to maximize the learning of other members?

   (5 minutes)

2. At the conclusion of the segment of the course, have the members of each quality circle collect and review the completed questionnaires. Each quality circle should summarize the group responses under three broad categories: "Helpful to Learning," "Not Helpful to Learning," "Changes to Facilitate Learning," noting participants' responses and suggestions for the facilitator. (15 minutes)

3. Provide each quality circle with acetate and marking pen. Each quality circle will select a recorder and a reporter. Members of each quality circle will prepare a presentation for the facilitator and other participants. They will be asked to prioritize the responses, making certain that at least two responses are addressed in each category. These priority responses are listed on acetate for total group viewing. (10 minutes)

4. Have the participants reconvene and each quality circle present their findings. Allow time for total group discussion. All reports are subsequently provided to the facilitator. (30 minutes)

Interpersonal Processes: Participant Observation. During the teaching and learning transaction, it is critical that all participants actively participate in order to maximize learning. Participation from a qualitative perspective is important and can be evaluated by a number of approaches.

As we believe that the type and distribution of leadership skills exhibited by all participants are crucial for groups to function effectively, we have chosen the evaluation strategy of participant observation. This strategy places the participants in a position to observe, critically analyze, and plan for the development of leadership skills, both for themselves individually and for other participants. Many methods of observation could be employed; we have chosen video-taping for this strategy. Wilson (1983) offers several suggestions for the use of technology in educational settings.

Leadership skills are applied in a group setting either as task behaviors (actions which are directly related to the attainment of group goals or objectives) or as maintenance behaviors (actions which are directly related to nurturance of group members and the intragroup processes that are operating). Six task and six maintenance behaviors provide an excellent vehicle for participant observation. The task behaviors are: information and opinion giver, information and opinion seeker, direction and role definer, summarizer, energizer, and comprehension checker. The maintenance behaviors are: encourager of participation, communication facilitator, tension releaser, process observer, interpersonal problem solver, and supporter and praiser (Johnson & Johnson, 1987).

The following steps should be employed in conducting the participant observation strategy:

1. Randomly select any small group project that will be occurring during the course and is no more than 15 minutes in length. Using a video tape recorder or camcorder, record the project. (15 minutes)

2. At the conclusion of the recording, assign each video-taped member a team chosen from the other participants. All participants should be assigned to a team. Provide all participants with a preprinted 8½ × 11 sheet with the twelve leadership behaviors listed on the left-hand side. Review the characteristics of the leadership behaviors with the participants. (5 minutes)

3. Instruct each team to observe only their video-taped team member during the replay of the recording and to tally on the preprinted sheet the number of times that person exhibits each of the twelve leadership behaviors. (5 minutes)

4. Replay the videotape. (15 minutes)

5. The team will discuss the behaviors tallied and select one well-developed leadership skill exhibited by the video-taped member, as well as one skill that could be improved. (10 minutes)

6. Have each video-taped member share what he or she learned with the entire group. (10 minutes)

Learning Climate: Problem-Solving Groups. The context or environment in which learning takes place has a definite effect upon the learner and facilitator. Mager (1968) has identified "five universal positives and negatives" which could provide valuable insights regarding learning climate. These universals are: physical comfort or physical discomfort, security or fear and anxiety, success or frustration, self-respect or humiliation and embarrassment, and involvement or boredom. Lewin, a German theoretician, has provided a problem-solving model, "force field analysis," through which we can both analyze and change a given situation. According to this model, all situations exist in a state of "dynamic equilibrium" because of positive and negative forces that impinge upon the situation. Positive forces drive change in a desired direction; negative forces restrain change from occurring in the desired direction. Eitington (1986) and Hall, Bowen, Lewicki, and Hall (1975) provide excellent examples of the application of force field analysis.

We feel that the learning climate could be best assessed by combining Lewin's force field analysis and Mager's five universal positives and negatives. Manipulation of these forces, as outlined by Lewin, can hold the key to effective change. First, the most potent negative forces should be eliminated or at least minimized; second, the strongest positive forces should be augmented; and last, forces of moderate to weak strength might be addressed as needed.

The following steps should be employed in conducting the problem-solving group strategy:

1. After the instructor explains Mager's model of the five universal positives and negatives, five color-coded, 3 × 5 index cards will be distributed to each participant, with each color representing one of the five universal positives and negatives. Have each participant draw a continuum on the appropriate colored card with the positive position at one end and the negative position at the other end. Have each participant place an "X" on the continuum which best represents his or her level of feeling and give one example of a factor associated with that feeling. (10 minutes)

2. Collect all individual index cards and place them in the five color-coded categories. Arrange members into five evaluation teams of no more than eight persons per team. Name each team after one of the universal positives or negatives and direct each team to appoint a recorder and a reporter. Distribute to each evaluation team the appropriate cards for their group. (5 minutes)

4. After explaining Lewin's theory to the entire group, instruct each team to analyze their cards and find the average positive for the entire group on the continuum. Each team will then analyze the group average according to force field analysis. Provide each team with newsprint and markers. Have them list several negative and positive factors, or forces, which impinge upon the learning situation and have contributed to the continuum findings. In addition, have each team list one strategy for improvement that the instructor may consider as the teaching and learning process continues. (30 minutes)

5. Each recorder will present the list prepared by the team to the entire group, with group discussion following. (15 minutes)

Strategies for Outgrowth Issues

Life Experiences: Buzz Groups. As we stated in the evaluation framework, outgrowth issues are inextricably linked to initiation issues. In the initiation issue concerned with life experiences we looked at prior life experiences. However, in looking at the life experiences of a learner as an outgrowth issue we are concerned with what was gained in the current learning situation. Was there personal or professional enrichment? Were new skills gained in interpersonal relationships? Was there any unanticipated learning?

We chose buzz groups for the evaluation strategy as they permit discussion in small groups as well as large groups, help identify needs and interests of participants, and allow for tapping into the ideas and feelings of introverted persons. Bergevin, Morris, and Smith (1963) offer a helpful discussion about employing buzz groups, as does Dickinson (1973). Buzz groups are most effective when coupled with a specific task. Completing an open-ended questionnaire serves as a specific task as well as allows for sharing personal development gained from the current learning situation.

The following steps should be employed in conducting the buzz group strategy:

1. Divide the participants into buzz groups of three or four persons each. Give each participant a copy of the open-ended questionnaire. Possible questions could include:

    —What do you personally feel you have gained from this class?

    —Do you feel that your interpersonal skills have improved? If so, how?

    —How was your life affected by taking this class? (positively or negatively)

    —What unexpected skills or knowledge did you acquire?

    (5 minutes)

2. Instruct each buzz group to select a recorder, complete the open-ended questionnaire individually, and then begin discussion of the questionnaire results. The recorder is to list, in brief statements, the various responses of each group member. (35 minutes)

3. Reconvene the group. Have each recorder share the results from his or her group. The instructor will list the results on the blackboard and complete the session with a short synopsis of the responses. (20 minutes)

Learning Style: Debate Teams. An important part of this outgrowth issue is knowing whether the learners benefitted from understanding personal learning styles or made modifications in their own learning styles. Since learning styles differ on an individual basis, and the differences can create disharmony between learners and instructor, it is important that all participants have the knowledge and ability to adapt to different learning situations. There are many practical applications of learning styles and learners should be familiar with these. Smith (1982) provides some helpful suggestions for application issues.

Part of our suggested evaluation strategy is a review of the *Group Embedded Figures Test* (GEFT) described in the evaluation of initiation issues. It is important that the participants reevaluate the results from the beginning of the course to determine if any modifications have taken place with their individual learning styles.

We chose debate teams as the strategy for evaluating this outgrowth issue, as debates are helpful in exploring various sides of an issue. It is not necessary to require a consensus, and when done in teams, everyone can participate. Debates also encourage or allow more than one avenue of thought. Several debate techniques are outlined in Eitington (1984).

The following steps should be employed in conducting the debate team strategy:

1. The instructor will pass out and review the results of the GEFT. Characteristics of each style (field dependent or field independent) should also be reviewed. (10 minutes)

2. The instructor will divide the group into two equal teams which will debate the benefits of knowing one's personal learning style. The debate issue will be: "Yes, I did benefit" versus "No, I did not benefit." The following questions should guide the teams in presenting sides of the issue:

   —Was it beneficial for me to know if I was field dependent or field independent?

—Was I able to make modificiations in my preferred style as the course progressed?

—Was I able to utilize any of the strategies for learning suggested by the other participants at the beginning of the course?

—Did it benefit me to know my instructor's style during this course?

—Will I be able to use this knowledge in the future?

(30 minutes)

3. The instructor should repeat each of the above questions to the entire group. A vote will be taken after each question, with the instructor tallying the results on the blackboard ("Yes" or "No"). Allow time for a brief discussion after the vote on each question. (20 minutes)

Course Expectations: Creative Activity. The evaluation strategy we have selected for course expectations is to readminister Pratt's Instructional Process/Environment Questionnaire (IPEQ). In the initiation issue related to course expectations we administered Pratt's instrument to determine the learner's preferences for the learning situation. In this section on outgrowth issues the IPEQ is used to assess the participant's actual learning experiences. This allows each participant to evaluate to what extent personal preferences were realized.

The determination of group satisfaction is as important as assessing individual satisfaction. A creative activity can be an excellent evaluation strategy. For example, the preparation of a marketing brochure is a creative activity that is fun, unites the group, allows for honest expression, and serves as an evaluative tool for the instructor in designing future learning experiences. A brochure is a strong indication of whether the course expectations were met, providing the instructor with immediate feedback. The brochure could be either positive or negative and might provide an outlet for the attitudes and feelings of each class member. Many other creative activities are suggested in Simon, Howe, and Kirschenbaum (1972) which could be used in the evaluation of course expectations.

The following steps should be employed in conducting the creative activity strategy:

1. Readminister and score the IPEQ, following the instructions provided by the instrument. (20 minutes)

2. Divide the participants into teams of four or five persons. Have each team develop an advertising brochure and select one member as a marketing representative. The brochure should reflect the satisfaction level of each person as indicated in the IPEQ scores, as well as serve as an advertisement for prospective students. It may encourage (or discourage) future enrollment. Provide each team with colored construction paper and markers for developing the brochure. Encourage creativity, spontaneity, and honesty. Make the project fun for participants. (20 minutes)

3. Reconvene the group. Have the marketing representative from each team "sell" the brochure to the entire group. (15 minutes)

4. Have each participant vote as to which marketing brochure best represents the course. The instructor may or may not collect the brochures. (5 minutes)

Future Planning: Panel/Role Play. The final outgrowth issue is future planning. As we explained earlier, this would be, for the instructor, a way to evaluate teaching strategies, spawn new ideas, or even motivate personal learning experiences. For the learners it may lead to new areas of learning and be an evaluation of how the learning experience impacted their lives.

One possible evaluation strategy that would expand on issues of future planning is that of role playing. Role playing promotes an atmosphere of creativity, along with individual participation. Insights into attitudes and behaviors are gained by the audience as well as the participants. It also helps in problem solving by providing skills and training. Bergevin, Morris, and Smith (1963) and Shaw (1967) are both sources with further explanation on the technique of role play. To promote group interaction, we suggest organizing role-playing panels. This enables all participants to have active input into the issues of future planning. Excellent sources that address the need for future planning and contain strategy ideas are Brinkerhoff (1987) and Hall, Bowen, Lewicki, and Hall (1975).

The following steps should be employed in conducting the panel/role play strategy:

1. Divide the participants into panels of four members each. Direct each panel to role play the part of the instructor and plan strategies for future courses, emphasizing personal and professional benefits for the learners. Provide each panel member with 5 × 8 cards to notate ideas generated. (15 minutes)

2. Each panel member will present a portion of the course outline to the entire group, role playing the part of instructor. Audience participants will respond as learners and give feedback to the panel. (30 minutes)

3. Group discussion, led by the instructor, will follow these activities. The discussion should focus on the individual learner's future planning. The instructor may also participate by sharing future plans. (15 minutes)

EVALUATION GUIDELINES

For the professional educator, evaluation can be a constant ally, but only when it has been shaped to suit each individual teaching and learning transaction. Consequently, we encourage each facilitator to develop an evaluation planning workbook. Over time, a workbook of strategies could meet many of the information needs which might be encountered. The workbook could contain

1. A listing of each of the central issues for evaluation

2. A listing of the criteria to consider for each evaluation strategy

3. At least one completely developed strategy for each issue identified which meets the most basic criteria of an egalitarian partnership and interactivity

4. A listing of how each strategy might be adapted to meet different time constraints, levels of group maturity, cultural sensitivities, literacy levels, and resource accessibilities

5. Results of prior evaluations and decisions made as a result of these evaluations

6. Additional strategy ideas which can be fully developed at a later time

In preparation for the development of the evaluation planning workbook, we encourage facilitators to review and assess how well their current evaluation strategies are meeting information and decision making needs. Not all strategies must be totally interactive, but those which are not and yet are important elements in the evaluation plan, should be reviewed for possible augmentation in order to maximize learning. An excellent source for each facilitator in future planning is *The Trainer's Guide to Andragogy* by John D. Ingalls (1973).

As it is possible to dedicate excessive time, energy, and resources to the evaluation process, decisions need to be made by each facilitator in devising the evaluation plan for each learning experience or program. Choices need to be made regarding the issues to be addressed in the evaluation process, and in the selection of those strategies which can best meet the needs in the present situation.

REFERENCES

Bergevin, P., Morris, D., & Smith, R. M. (1963). *Adult education procedures: Handbook of tested patterns for effective participation*. New York: Seabury.

Bonham, L. A. (1988). Learning style instruments: Let the buyer beware. *Lifelong Learning: An Omnibus of Practice and Research, 11*(6), 12–16.

Brinkerhoff, R. O. (1987). *Achieving results from training: How to evaluate human resource development to strengthen programs and increase impact*. San Francisco: Jossey-Bass.

Brundage, D. H., & Mackeracher, D. (1980). *Adult learning principles and their application to program planning*. Toronto, Ontario, Canada: Ontario Institute for Studies in Education.

Canfield, A. A. (1983). *Canfield learning styles inventory, form S-A manual*. Birmingham: Humanics Media.

Casner-Lotto, J. and Associates. (1988). *Successful training strategies*. San Francisco: Jossey-Bass.

Darkenwald, G., & Valentine, T. (1986). Measuring the social environment of adult education classrooms. *Proceedings of the Twenty-Seventh Annual Adult Education Research Conference* (pp. 77–81). Syracuse: Syracuse University.

Deshler, D. (Ed.). (1984). *Evaluation for program improvement.* New Directions for Continuing Education, no. 24. San Francisco: Jossey-Bass.

Dickinson, G. (1973). *Teaching adults: A handbook for instructors.* Oshawa, Ontario, Canada: Alger.

Eitington, J. E. (1984). *The winning trainer.* Houston: Gulf.

Forsyth, D. R. (1983). *An introduction to group dynamics.* Monterey: Brooks/Cole.

French-Lazovik, G. (Ed.). (1982). *Practices that improve teaching evaluation.* New Directions for Teaching and Learning, no. 11. San Francisco: Jossey-Bass.

Hall, D. T., Bowen, D. D., Lewicki, R. J., & Hall, F. S. (1975). *Experiences in management and organizational behavior.* Chicago: St. Clair.

Herman, J. L. (Ed.). (1987). *Program evaluation kit* (Vols. 1–9). Newbury Park: Sage.

Ingalls, J. D. (1973). *A trainers guide to andragogy.* Waltham: Data Education.

Johnson, D. W., & Johnson, F. P. (1987). *Joining together: Group theory and group skills.* Englewood Cliffs: Prentice-Hall.

Kolb, D. A. (1976). *Learning style inventory technical manual.* Boston: McBer.

Mager, R. F. (1968). *Developing attitude toward learning.* Belmont: Lear Siegler, Inc./Fearon.

Oltman, P. K., Raskin, E., & Witkin, H. A. (1971). *Group embedded figures test.* Palo Alto: Consulting Psychologists.

Pratt, D. D. (1979). Instructor behavior and psychological climate in adult learning. In *Twentieth Annual Adult Education Research Conference Proceedings* (pp. 106–115). Ann Arbor: University of Michigan.

Rosenblum, S. H. (Ed.). (1985). *Involving adults in the educational process.* New Directions for Continuing Education, no. 26. San Francisco: Jossey-Bass.

Schmeck, R. R., & Ribich, F. D. (1978). Construct validation of the inventory of learning processes. *Applied Psychological Measurement, 2,* 551–562.

Schmeck, R. R., Ribich, F., & Ramanaiah, N. (1977). Development of a self-report inventory for assessing individual differences in learning processes. *Applied Psychological Measurement, 1,* 413–431.

Seaman, D. F., & Fellenz, R. A. (1989). *Effective strategies for teaching adults*. Columbus: Merrill.

Shaw, M. E. (1967). Role playing. In R. L. Craig & L. R. Bittel (Eds.), *Training and development handbook* (pp. 206–224). New York: McGraw-Hill.

Simon, S. B., Howe, L. W., & Kirschenbaum, H. (1972). *Values clarification: A handbook of practical strategies for teachers and students*. New York: Hart.

Smith, R. M. (1982). *Learning how to learn: Applied theory for adults*. Chicago: Follett.

Wilson, J. P. (Ed.). (1983). *Materials for teaching adults: Selection, development, and use*. New Directions for Continuing Education, no. 17. San Francisco: Jossey-Bass.

Witkin, H. A. (1976). Cognitive style in academic performance and in teacher-student relations. In S. Messick & Associates, *Individuality in learning* (pp. 38–72). San Francisco: Jossey-Bass.

Witkin, H. A., Moore, C. A., Goodenough, D. R., & Cox, P. W. (1977). Field-dependent and field-independent cognitive styles and their educational implications. *Review of Educational Research, 47*(1), 1–64.

CHAPTER 8

Strategies and Resources for Improving the Instructional Process

RALPH G. BROCKETT

By now, it should be clear that the process of helping adults learn is very complex. It takes a special person to effectively facilitate this process. Phrases such as "anyone can teach, anyone can learn" (Draves, 1984) and "friends teaching friends" (Cunningham, 1988) are sometimes used as a way of demystifying the instructional process. However, if accepted literally and uncritically, slogans such as these can be harmful if accepted by those who see little value in learning about teaching. On the other hand, if these phrases are used to illustrate that each of us has the *potential* to work effectively with adult learners, then they take on a very different meaning.

The purpose of this chapter is to present an array of strategies and resources that facilitators of adult learning can draw upon in order to improve the instructional process. The first part of the chapter will examine several practical strategies for improving instruction. The second part will present an annotated bibliography of resources that offer insights into various aspects of the instructional process.

The ideas that follow are based on two assumptions. First, ongoing professional development is an important element of a person's responsibility as a facilitator of adult learning. The field of adult education is growing and changing at a rapid pace. Those who wish to stay on the cutting edge of new programs and practices

193

therefore need to develop an active plan for continuous professional development. Previously, I have stated that keeping up with new developments in the field is more than a luxury—it is a necessity (Brockett, 1986). I would expand this now to state that keeping up is a *responsibility* and is central to what we do as educators of adults.

Second, a major purpose of professional development is to help adult educators to critically reflect upon their practice. The word *critical* has come to be used very widely in educational circles in recent years. Critical thinking is viewed as a major skill to be taught in schools, critical reflection is a vital element of the human development process, and critical theory has emerged as an important paradigm for understanding human liberation and empowerment. In each case, the use of the word stresses that there are many, often conflicting, ways of looking at any given situation. The educator who engages in critical reflection, then, is involved in a process of examining these differing views of reality and, in doing so, is defining the nature of the problem. As Cervero (1988) points out, the problems of professional practice are generally messy and ambiguous; thus, "problem setting rather than problem solving is the key to professional practice" (p. 31). What this means for those who facilitate adult learning is that it is important to continuously search for different ways of looking at a given situation. By doing so and by reflecting on the strengths and weaknesses of each view, it should be possible to arrive at new and innovative ways of thinking about a problem.

STRATEGIES FOR IMPROVING THE INSTRUCTIONAL PROCESS

There are many strategies through which facilitators of adult learning can engage in reflective practice and work toward fulfilling their responsibilities as professionals. For instance, Apps (1985) suggests that reading, participating in the arts, thinking, writing, discussing, and taking action can be helpful ways to analyze practice. In this chapter, the following strategies will be considered: reading, writing, professional associations, electronic networks, and courses in adult education.

Reading

Perhaps the most obvious strategy for improving instruction is professional reading. Reading is convenient and easy to adapt to a busy schedule. Among the potential benefits of reading professional literature are (1) developing new knowledge; (2) sharing new information and ideas; (3) promoting critical thinking; and (4) fostering professional socialization and reaffirmation. While each of these benefits can be achieved through each of the strategies discussed in this chapter, reading is perhaps the most flexible and least costly of these approaches.

In a previous article, I presented four strategies for incorporating professional reading into a personal professional development agenda (Brockett, 1986). First, it is important to take a *proactive attitude* toward reading. Simply stated, this means that "rather than being a one-way transmission of information," reading can be a strategy for self-directed inquiry (Knowles, 1975, p. 105). Second, it is often possible to gain even more from reading through *sharing* with others. One vehicle for accomplishing this is the study group or journal club. Such groups can be very informal in their operation or they can be highly structured, even to the point of awarding continuing education units (CEUs) for participation (e.g., Kranstuber, 1982). In any case, the study group provides an outlet where people with common interests and concerns can meet to exchange ideas and interact with one another. Third, it is important to overcome the urge to rely upon one or two primary publications for ideas and, instead, to *read widely* from a variety of sources. We must not assume that because a journal appears to be directed toward a specific clientele it has nothing to say to readers outside these areas. The *Journal of Continuing Education in Nursing* and the *Journal of Extension,* for example, often include articles that offer valuable insights to facilitators of adult learning who work outside these fields. Finally, it is important to invest time and energy in the *planning* and continuous evaluation of a reading agenda. In addition to a greater return on the investment, conscious planning can help us to set aside time in the work schedule for such activity.

The professional literature of adult education is growing rapidly. As this happens, it is becoming increasingly important to know how to access or locate appropriate literature. Imel (1989) discusses several libraries, information data bases, and clearinghouses that are among the most valuable information sources for educators of adults. Perhaps the most important of these is the Educational Resources Information Center (ERIC). Imel describes ERIC as follows:

> Currently funded by the U.S. Department of Education's Office of Educational Research and Improvement, ERIC is designed to put the results of educational research into the hands of researchers, practitioners, policymakers, and others interested in information about education. Since 1966, ERIC has been collecting and classifying all types of educational materials. . . . More than 700 education-related journals are scanned regularly to select articles for inclusion in ERIC, including all major adult education journals. (p. 141)

ERIC can be searched in several ways. First, one can manually search the two bimonthly indexes: *Resources in Education* (RIE) and *Current Index to Journals in Education* (CIJE). RIE includes a listing of "fugitive" materials (that is, resources that have not been published elsewhere such as working papers, speeches, or unpublished conference papers) that have been processed into the ERIC collection. Items listed in RIE can typically be found on microform in libraries designated as depositories for ERIC. CIJE is an index of articles that have recently been published in education-related journals. Since these articles have been published elsewhere, they are not available on microform through ERIC; one must go to the actual publication in which the article appears. Both RIE and CIJE include abstracts of each publication indexed.

Second, ERIC can be searched by a trained searcher. The advantage here is that librarians trained in computer searching can often help clients identify key words and phrases that will simplify the search process. The main disadvantage is that there is a charge for such searches, although the cost for a computer search of ERIC is typically considerably less than for many other databases.

Third, in recent years, ERIC has been made available on CD-ROM (compact disk–read only memory). For those with access to this option, it is possible to do personal searches from a microcomputer and avoid the charges of a professional search. The advantages and disadvantages of this option are essentially the opposite of those for a professional search.

Imel estimates that since 1966, "more than 12,500 items whose major topic is related to adult education have been selected for inclusion in the ERIC data base" (p. 141). Whether we are looking for specific information about a particular topic or simply seeking to stay on top of current developments in the field, ERIC is an invaluable tool. Best of all, it is accessible and easy to learn.

Writing

Writing is another strategy for critical reflection. By putting our thoughts down on paper, a lasting record of thoughts, feelings, and ideas has been created. Looking back on our earlier ideas and perceptions is an invaluable part of the critical reflection process.

Writing can be viewed as a tool for improving instruction at two levels: personal writing intended only for the writer and public writing intended to be shared with others. Perhaps the most obvious example of the first type of writing is the personal journal or log. Progoff (1975) discusses what he refers to as the "intensive journal" process. In this process, the writer engages in a dialectical movement between personal experiences and reflections upon those experiences. While Progoff describes the intensive journal as a therapeutic process designed for individual personal growth, it can easily be adopted by adult educators for the more specific purpose of improving instruction. By keeping a journal, where descriptions of what takes place in the instructional setting are combined with reflection and analysis of the events, it is possible to gain new and valuable insights. This is the essence of the journal process.

Personal philosophy statements are another example of this first type of writing. Each of us has a philosophy that guides how we practice as facilitators of adult learning; yet, many of us do not actually sit down and spell out what this philosophy actually *is*. As Apps (1985) has pointed out, analyzing our priorities and practices as adult educators can help us to "see our experience in a fresh way" (p. 6); to see alternative ways of practicing; to become aware of values, ethics, and esthetics related to the education of adults; to reflect upon the past and future; and to be freed from "depending on someone else's doctrine" (p. 7). By spelling out a personal philosophy of adult education, each of us will have articulated a doctrine. This, then, can be used as a yardstick against which practice can be measured. And perhaps most important, since a personal philosophy is a "working" philosophy, it is not concrete; rather, it is subject to modification as we gain and reflect upon new experiences. Hiemstra (1988) provides a useful description of how we can develop a statement of personal philosophy.

Writing for publication is another useful tool for improving instruction. The notion that only academicians can publish is a very harmful misconception. While publishing is, in fact, most often linked with the academic world, practitioners offer a perspective that is different from and often complementary to the academic viewpoint. Quite simply, our field needs to have more writing from practitioners. The potential benefits of writing are many. First, there is the sense of personal satisfaction that comes from the creative process. Second, publishing can bring visibility and prestige to the author's institution. Third, writing for publication can be an important technique for self-education. Fourth, publishing provides a way of sharing ideas with others in the field; thus, it can help practitioners elsewhere avoid duplication of effort. Apps (1982) and Becker (1986) offer some ideas on writing for publication. Other helpful sources can include the guidelines for authors that appear in many journals, as well as conference sessions on writing for publication.

Professional Associations and Conferences

Professional associations serve a vital function in the field of adult education. Through such associations, individuals come together to "to furnish collaborative leadership" to the field (Fellenz, 1981, p. 228). In other words, professional associations provide a vision for the adult education field while simultaneously serving as a valuable source of professional development for those who practice in the field. Indeed, Darkenwald and Merriam (1982) have suggested that opportunities for professional development may be the single most important function of associations. In addition, associations can offer other benefits by contributing to the identity of the field and by providing advocacy for adult education throughout society.

In adult education, professional associations exist on local, state/provincial, regional, national, and international levels. Some associations see their role as providing an "umbrella" through which various segments of the field can be unified. Others see their role as serving a specific segment of the field such as adult basic education, continuing higher education, or training and development (Brockett, 1989).

Adult educators who seek to use associations as a vehicle for professional development should consider what they hope to gain through such affiliations. For instance, local associations tend to focus on the concerns of a specific community. State (and provincial) associations often play an active role in influencing legislation relative to adult education. Regional associations typically address common concerns throughout a specific geographical region; these associations are especially important to practitioners who may not be able to afford membership and/or conference fees in national associations. At the national level, particular emphasis is placed on creating the vision of a coordinated adult education field. And, as has been suggested elsewhere,

> Because these associations have a broad-based membership, they have a resource base much broader than local, state, or regional groups. Publications, education, and legislative relations are three of the major services of these associations. (Brockett, 1989, p. 118)

Finally, international associations deal with issues that are much more global in nature. The person who wishes to actively incorporate association involvement into a professional development plan would be well advised to consider membership in several types of associations, devoting the greatest amount of time and energy to the groups that seem to be most consistent with personal professional goals, interests, and focus.

Conferences are one of the most important activities of professional associations. Benefits of attending conferences include opportunities for the following:

- To meet others with shared interests and concerns about working with adult learners

- To learn about new practices and ideas

- To share ideas and experiences, either informally or as a formal presentation

- To reaffirm a commitment to the field of adult education

Experienced conference-goers know that such gatherings, especially at the national or regional levels, can be something of a smorgasbord, with a need to select activities from a wide range of possibilities. Thus, as with any other professional development ac-

tivity, it is wise to have a plan of action when attending a conference. Some individuals take a tracking approach to conferencing,
where they attempt to spend their time in activities related to a
specific program area or theme, for example, older adults, adult
basic education, evaluation, or teaching adults. Tracking can be an
effective strategy, especially for people who have very clear goals in
attending a conference. However, those who are new to an association or to conferencing in general might want to consider a sampling approach, which will allow more of a chance to capture the
overall flavor or spirit of the gathering. In any case, whether we
choose a tracking approach, a sampling approach, or some combination of the two, the benefits derived from conference attendance
are likely to be greater if we consider in advance what we hope to
gain from the experience.

Electronic Networks

Study groups, professional associations, and conferences provide excellent opportunities for face-to-face networking with colleagues. However, these approaches only allow for periodic contact. In recent years, electronic networks have begun to play an
increasingly important role in professional development. Simply
stated, individuals who have access to an electronic network, a
computer, and a modem can—from the convenience of their home
or office—communicate with another member of the network
whenever they choose to do so. While electronic networks do not
allow for the advantages of face-to-face communication nor the
spontaneous interchange of the telephone, they are perhaps the next
best thing and can do much to reduce long distance telephone bills,
often made larger by missed connections.

An example of an electronic network developed specifically
for adult educators is the Adult Education Network (AEDNET)
operated by the Kellogg Project at Syracuse University. Operating
via BITNET, an electronic mail network, AEDNET offers such services as forums on topics of current interest in the field, an electronic bulletin board, and a journal managed by graduate students,
New Horizons in Adult Education. As of spring 1990, AEDNET
had over two hundred participants from North America and several
other continents.

To date, the one drawback of electronic networks is that participants must have access to an electronic mail system such as

BITNET. Typically, such programs are linked to mainframe computers in universities and large corporations. Thus, access to such a mainframe computer is necessary to access the system. Since many people who work with adult learners currently do not have such access, electronic networking may not be a viable option at present. However, as the technology expands and new types of networks become available, this method of communication is likely to become much more commonplace.

From a personal perspective, electronic mail has had a major impact upon my own professional activity. During a two and a half year period, I have used electronic mail to do the following:

- To keep up informal networks with colleagues throughout North America and other continents

- To work with a co-author, separated by over two thousand miles, on a book project

- To work with a doctoral advisee on the completion and defense of a dissertation

- To communicate with authors and editors in my capacity as an editor and editorial board member

- To communicate with others in my capacity as a board member with a professional association

- To serve as participant and moderator for AEDNET-sponsored forums on issues related to adult education

Speaking as one person, the benefits of electronic networking have been tremendous. Electronic mail is a medium that can increase opportunities for networking with others in a much more timely and cost efficient manner than by mail or telephone.

Courses in Adult Education

One final strategy for improving the instructional process is through formal courses in adult education. Since 1922, when the phrase *adult education* first appeared in a course offered at Teachers College, Columbia University (Houle, 1964), the number of programs offering degrees in adult education has steadily grown. Jones and Galbraith (1985) reported that 165 colleges and universities in the United States and Canada offered coursework and/or degree programs in adult education. An anthology by Brookfield (1988) offers insights into the historical development and current issues facing the formal preparation of professional adult educators. For the most part, courses and degree programs in adult education are found at the masters or doctoral level; however, some institutions across North America do offer undergraduate courses. Although critics of undergraduate courses in adult education believe that professional preparation in the field should be reserved for the graduate level, undergraduate offerings have the potential to encourage individuals to make a commitment to the field much earlier in their careers.

While cost and time commitments are sometimes seen as barriers to enrollment in formal courses, the following potential benefits can clearly outweigh the barriers:

- There are opportunities to establish informal networks with other adult educators.

- Participants have a chance to gain a broad perspective on the field of adult education and to better understand where they fit within the big picture.

- Courses can provide exposure to some of the most current research and thinking on adult education.

- A degree in adult education can open new doors for professional opportunity.

When considering coursework in adult education, it is important to remember that there is great diversity in programs. They will vary considerably in such areas as course offerings, faculty size, methods of delivery, and areas of specialization. In an effort to define common ground for graduate programs in adult education, the Commission of Professors of Adult Education (n.d.) recently established a set of standards for graduate programs. This document offers guidelines for graduate programs in adult education in the areas of curriculum, faculty, organization of graduate study, students' programs, resources and facilities, and scholarship. (NOTE: These standards can be obtained from the American Association for Adult and Continuing Education, 1112 16th Street, N.W., Suite 420, Washington, D.C. 20036.)

RESOURCES FOR IMPROVING INSTRUCTION

There has been a tremendous growth in resources related to the education of adults in recent years. Indeed, it is beyond the scope of this chapter to provide a comprehensive bibliography of these resources. However, this section will offer an annotated bibliography of several key works that should be helpful for facilitators of adult learning. The twenty-five works selected for inclusion here are intended to reflect a range of practice versus theory-oriented publications, and stress both recent and classic writings on facilitating adult learning. In addition, a list of major periodicals in adult learning is included.

Books

Apps, J. W. (1985). *Improving practice in continuing education.* San Francisco: Jossey-Bass.

Offers an approach for systematically analyzing practices in the education of adults. Includes new ways of thinking about adult learners, the teaching and learning process, and program development.

Brockett, R. G. (Ed.). (1988). *Ethical issues in adult education.* New York: Teachers College Press.

Addresses the often-overlooked topic of ethics relative to the education of adults. Chapters cover a wide range of practice areas and issues including: program planning, marketing, administration, evaluation, teaching, advising and brokering, ethical development, social responsibility, research, code of ethics, and development of a personal philosophy.

Brockett, R. G., & Hiemstra, R. (1991). *Self-direction in adult learning: Perspectives in theory, research, and practice.* London and New York: Routledge.

Examines one of the most widely studied topics in adult education over the past two decades. Offers a model for distinguishing between self-direction as a personality characteristic and as an instructional process and includes an extensive review of research and applications to practice.

Brookfield, S. D. (1986). *Understanding and facilitating adult learning*. San Francisco: Jossey-Bass.

Provides a comprehensive critical analysis of facilitating adult learning. Major themes include how adults learn, facilitating adult learning, and program development.

Brookfield, S. D. (1987). *Developing critical thinkers*. San Francisco: Jossey-Bass.

Critical thinking has come to be viewed as a vital goal for learning across the lifespan. This book provides an insightful treatment of critical thinking relative to adult learners and offers practical strategies for helping adults develop critical thinking skills.

Cross, K. P. (1981). *Adults as learners*. San Francisco: Jossey-Bass.

Generally considered to be one of the most important works on adult learning of the 1980s. While much of the research reported in the book is becoming outdated, the book still offers a clear synthesis of research prior to 1980.

Daloz, L. A. (1986). *Effective teaching and mentoring*. San Francisco: Jossey-Bass.

Discusses the idea of education as a "transformational journey." In stressing the importance of adult development on learning, the book offers strategies for helping adult learners on this journey.

Draves, W. A. (1984). *How to teach adults*. Manhattan, KS: LERN.

A practical guide of particular interest to those new to teaching adults. Includes information about adult learners, tips for course planning, and strategies for improving teaching techniques.

Elias, J. L., & Merriam, S. (1980). *Philosophical foundations of adult education*. Malabar: FL: Krieger.

A clearly written overview of major philosophies in adult education. Offers comparisons and contrasts among liberal, progressive, behaviorist, humanist, radical, and analytical views of adult education that can be useful to readers who wish to assess their approach to adult education.

Galbraith, M. W. (Ed.). (1990). *Adult learning methods: A guide for effective instruction.* Malabar, FL: Krieger.

A series of original contributions that provide insights on understanding and facilitating adult learning. Includes detailed chapters devoted to specific methods and techniques that can be used in helping adults learn.

Hayes, E. (Ed.). (1989). *Effective teaching styles.* New Directions for Continuing Education, no. 43. San Francisco: Jossey-Bass.

This sourcebook considers the importance of teaching style in the education of adults. Drawing from recent theory and research, the book provides tools and strategies for using teaching style to enhance adult learning.

Hiemstra, R., & Sisco, B. R. (1990). *Individualizing instruction: Making learning personal, empowering, and successful.* San Francisco: Jossey-Bass.

This book offers an innovative approach for individualizing the teaching-learning process. Includes many practical strategies for facilitating a process emphasizing the individualizing of instruction.

Jarvis, P. (1987). *Adult learning in the social context.* London: Croom Helm.

This book looks at adult learning from a sociological perspective. While the book has a strong orientation toward theory, ideas related to social context and reflective learning have important implications for facilitators of adult learning.

Kidd, J. R. (1973). *How adults learn.* New York: Cambridge.

A classic work on adult learning. Although somewhat dated, the book still includes valuable insights on such areas as the affective domain, environmental factors in learning, and the learning transaction.

Knowles, M. S. (1980). *The modern practice of adult education: From andragogy to pedagogy.* New York: Cambridge.

Knowles's classic work on program development for adults includes a clear discussion of andragogy as a model for helping adults learn. One of the most important books ever published on North American adult education.

Knowles, M. S. (1988). *The adult learner: A neglected species* (4th ed.). Houston: Gulf.

A further elaboration of Knowles's ideas on facilitating adult learning, this book emphasizes the application of teaching and learning theories to practice. Special emphasis is placed on the human resource development context, though the book is relevant to teachers of adults in other settings as well.

Knowles, M. S., and Associates. (1984). *Andragogy in action.* San Francisco: Jossey-Bass.

This book includes case studies of programs where principles of andragogy have been effectively utilized. Includes applications to programs in business, industry, and government; colleges and universities; professions; religious institutions; elementary and secondary education; and remedial education.

Knox, A. B. (1986). *Helping adults learn.* San Francisco: Jossey-Bass.

Presents strategies for planning, implementing, and evaluating programs for adult learners. Stresses the overall program development process as opposed to just the teaching-learning transaction.

Lindeman, E. C. (1989). *The meaning of adult education.* Norman, OK: Oklahoma Research Center for Continuing Higher and Professional Education.

Originally published in 1926, this work remains an enduring classic in the field because of its inspirational tone and its emphasis on the importance of the learner's experience in the educational process.

Merriam, S. B. (Ed.). (1986). *Being responsive to adult learners.* Glenview, IL: Scott, Foresman and Company.

This brief (50-page) book consists of eleven articles or excerpts of articles previously published in *Lifelong Learning* and *Adult Education Quarterly.* A useful guide for beginning teachers and a helpful supplemental resource for more experienced educators.

Merriam, S. B., & Cunningham, P. M. (Eds). (1989). *Handbook of adult and continuing education.* San Francisco: Jossey-Bass.

A comprehensive look at the current adult education field in North America. Includes chapters by leaders from throughout the field on such areas as professional practice, adult learners and the educational process, providers of educational programs for adults, program areas and special clienteles, and the future of the field.

Seaman, D. F., & Fellenz, R. A. (1989). *Effective strategies for teaching adults.* Columbus, OH: Merrill.

This book identifies and reviews specific techniques for teaching adults. The authors discuss presentation, action, and interaction strategies and touch on selected characteristics of adult learning.

Smith, R. M. (1982). *Learning how to learn.* New York: Cambridge.

In this book, Smith argues that a key to helping others learn involves helping them learn *how* to learn. The book includes an overview of the adult learner and learning styles, strategies for helping learners develop skills for learning in a wide range of settings, and ideas for providing training on learning how to learn.

Verner, C. (1962). *A conceptual scheme for the identification of classifications and processes.* Washington, DC: Adult Education Association of the U.S.A.

This 34-page monograph was an attempt to clarify major concepts in adult education. Especially important is Verner's distinction among methods, techniques, and devices in teaching adults.

Wlodkowski, R. J. (1985). *Enhancing adult motivation to learn.* San Francisco: Jossey-Bass.

An extensive look at the importance of motivation in adult learning. The author proposes a model suggesting that different strategies will be most effective at the beginning, middle, and end of a learning activity and includes many practical strategies for enhancing motivation.

Periodicals

Adult Education Quarterly
This publication of the American Association for Adult and Continuing Education (AAACE) is the major research journal for adult education in North America.

Adult Learning
This magazine, which is published eight times per year by AAACE, includes articles and feature columns designed particularly for adult education practitioners.

Adult Basic Education: An Interdisciplinary Journal for Adult Literacy Educators
Published three times per year by the Commission on Adult Basic Education of AAACE, this journal is committed to improving educational practice of those adult educators working in the literacy field.

Community Education Journal
Published quarterly by the Community Education Association (CEA), this journal emphasizes current trends, issues, and practices in community education.

Convergence
Emphasizing developments in adult education throughout the world, with an emphasis on developing countries, this quarterly journal is published by the International Council for Adult Education (ICAE).

Educational Gerontology
An international bimonthly journal for adult educators who develop educational programs for older adults or for professionals in the gerontology field.

International Journal of Lifelong Education
A quarterly journal designed to provide an international forum for discussion of problems and practices related to lifelong education.

Journal of Continuing Education in Nursing
While directed primarily toward continuing education professionals in the nursing field, this periodical often includes informative ideas on teaching and program development.

Journal of Extension
A practitioner-oriented publication for extension professionals, this journal is described in its editorial guidelines as being for "active professionals who take a few minutes out of a busy schedule" for professional reading.

MPAEA Journal of Adult Education
Published by the Mountain Plains Adult Education Association, this is perhaps the strongest regional adult education journal in North America.

New Directions for Adult and Continuing Education
A quarterly sourcebook series published by Jossey-Bass. Each sourcebook focuses on a specific theme and includes chapters designed to bridge theory and practice.

New Horizons in Adult Education
A unique publication in adult education for two reasons: first, it is the first electronic journal in the field, distributed through Syracuse University's AEDNET and second, because it is entirely managed by graduate students.

Training
A magazine geared toward human resource development professionals, which often includes articles of interest to teachers of adults.

Training and Development Journal
Published by the American Society for Training and Development, this journal includes articles related specifically to the training and development field.

CONCLUSION

Adult education is a rapidly changing field. One need only look at the ideas presented in the previous chapters in order to gain a sense that the field is evolving continuously. Many of the ideas discussed earlier are the product of developments that have taken place during the past twenty years or so. It is clear that rapid change will continue to be central to adult education as we move toward the year 2000.

It is not enough to stay aware of new developments in the field. This implies a passive approach to practice, where we are merely *reacting* to changes. Instead, it makes sense for each of us to think in terms of working to *create* the kind of future we desire for the field. Improving the instructional process implies a desire and willingness to think about the future and to take steps that will allow each of us to have a part in creating that future.

REFERENCES

Apps, J. W. (1982). *Improving your writing skills*. New York: Cambridge.

Apps, J. W. (1985). *Improving practice in continuing education*. San Francisco: Jossey-Bass.

Becker, H. S. (1986). *Writing for social scientists*. Chicago: University of Chicago Press.

Brockett, R. G. (1986). Keeping up with professional reading is more than a luxury. *Community Education Journal, 13*(3), 9–11.

Brockett, R. G. (Ed.). (1988). *Ethical issues in adult education.* New York: Teachers College Press.

Brockett, R. G. (1989). Professional associations for adult and continuing eduction. In S. B. Merrian & P. M. Cunningham (Eds.), *Handbook of adult and continuing education* (pp. 112–123). San Francisco: Jossey-Bass.

Brockett, R. G., & Hiemstra, R. (1991). *Self-direction in adult learning: Perspectives in theory, research, and practice.* London and New York: Routledge.

Brookfield, S. D. (1986). *Understanding and facilitating adult learning.* San Francisco: Jossey-Bass.

Brookfield, S. D. (1987). *Developing critical thinkers.* San Francisco: Jossey-Bass.

Brookfield, S. D. (Ed.). (1988). *Training educators of adults.* London and New York: Routledge.

Cervero, R. M. (1988). *Effective continuing education for professionals.* San Francisco: Jossey-Bass.

Commission of Professors of Adult Education. (n.d.). *Standards for graduate programs in adult education.* Washington, DC: American Association for Adult and Continuing Education.

Cross, K. P. (1981). *Adults as learners.* San Francisco: Jossey-Bass.

Cunningham, P. M. (1988). The adult educator and social responsibility. In R. G. Brockett (Ed.), *Ethical issues in adult education* (pp. 133–145). New York: Teachers College Press.

Daloz, L. A. (1986). *Effective teaching and mentoring.* San Francisco: Jossey-Bass.

Darkenwald, G. G., & Merriam, S. B.(1982). *Adult education: Foundations of practice.* New York: Harper & Row.

Draves, W. A. (1984). *How to teach adults.* Manhattan, KS: LERN.

Elias, J. L., & Merriam, S. (1980). *Philosophical foundations of adult education.* Malabar FL: Krieger.

Fellenz, R. A. (1981). The national leadership role belongs to professional adult educators. In B. W. Kreitlow (Ed.), *Examining controversies in adult education* (pp. 215–233). San Francisco: Jossey-Bass.

Galbraith, M. W. (Ed.). (1990). *Adult learning methods: A guide for effective instruction.* Malabar, FL: Krieger.

Hayes, E. (Ed.). (1989). *Effective teaching styles.* New Directions for Continuing Education, no. 43. San Francisco: Jossey-Bass.

Hiemstra, R. (1988). Translating personal values and philosophy into practical action. In R. G. Brockett (Ed.), *Ethical issues in adult education* (pp. 178–194). New York: Teachers College Press.

Hiemstra, R., & Sisco, B. R. (1990). *Individualizing instruction: Making learning personal, empowering, and successful.* San Francisco: Jossey-Bass.

Houle, C. O. (1964). The emergence of graduate study in adult education. In G. Jensen, A. A. Liveright, & W. Hallenbeck (Eds.), *Adult education: Outlines of an emerging field of university study* (pp. 69–83). Washington, DC: Adult Education Association of the U.S.A.

Imel, S. (1989). The field's literature and information sources. In S. B. Merriam & P. M. Cunningham (Eds.), *Handbook of adult and continuing education* (pp. 134–146). San Francisco: Jossey-Bass.

Jarvis, P. (1987). *Adult learning in the social context.* London: Croom Helm.

Jones, G. E., & Galbraith, M. W. (1985). *Adult education: A study of graduate programs in the United States and Canada.* Unpublished manuscript.

Kidd, J. R. (1973). *How adults learn.* New York: Cambridge.

Knowles, M. S. (1975). *Self-directed learning.* Chicago: Follett.

Knowles, M. S. (1980). *The modern practice of adult education: From andragogy to pedagogy.* New York: Cambridge.

Knowles, M. S. (1988). *The adult learner: A neglected species* (4th ed). Houston: Gulf.

Knowles, M. S., and Associates. (1984). *Andragogy in action.* San Francisco: Jossey-Bass.

Knox, A. B. (1986). *Helping adults learn.* San Francisco: Jossey-Bass.

Kranstuber, S. S. M. (1982). Establishing a nursing journal club for professional education and certification. *Journal of Continuing Education in Nursing, 13* (January/February), 24–27.

Lindeman, E. C. (1989). *The meaning of adult education.* Norman, OK: Oklahoma Research Center for Continuing Higher and Professional Education.

Merriam, S. B. (Ed.). (1986). *Being responsive to adult learners.* Glenview, IL: Scott, Foresman and Company.

Merriam, S. B., & Cunningham, P. M. (Eds). (1989). *Handbook of adult and continuing education.* San Francisco: Jossey-Bass.

Progoff, I. (1975). *At a journal workshop.* New York: Dialogue House Library.

Seaman, D. F., & Fellenz, R. A. (1989). *Effective strategies for teaching adults.* Columbus, OH: Merrill.

Smith, R. M. (1982). *Learning how to learn.* New York: Cambridge.

Verner, C. (1962). *A conceptual scheme for the identification of classifications and processes.* Washington, DC: Adult Education Association of the U.S.A.

Wlodkowski, R. J. (1985). *Enhancing adult motivation to learn.* San Francisco: Jossey-Bass.

Index